THE
LIBRARY OF
CONGRESS

Other Books by Gene Gurney

The Air Force Museum
(coauthored with Nick Apple)

Agriculture Careers

America in Wax

Americans into Orbit

Americans to the Moon

Arlington National Cemetery

Beautiful Washington, D.C.

The B-29 Story

Chronology of World Aviation

Cosmonauts in Orbit

Five Down and Glory

Flying Aces of World War I

Flying Minutemen—The Story
of the Civil Air Patrol

Great Air Battles

Guide to U.S. Service and
Maritime Academies

Handbook to Successful
Franchising

How to Save Your Life on the
Nation's Highways and Byways

Journey of the Giants

Kingdoms of the World

The Library of Congress

Maryland

Monticello

Mount Vernon

North and South Korea

The Official Washington, D.C.,
Directory

The Pentagon

The Pictorial History of the
U.S. Army

Private Pilot's Handbook of
Navigation

Private Pilot's Handbook of
Weather

The P-38 Lightning

Rocket and Missile Technology

The Smithsonian Institution

Space Age Technology

Test Pilots

Unidentified Flying Objects

Walk in Space—The Story of
Project Gemini

The War in the Air

Women on the March

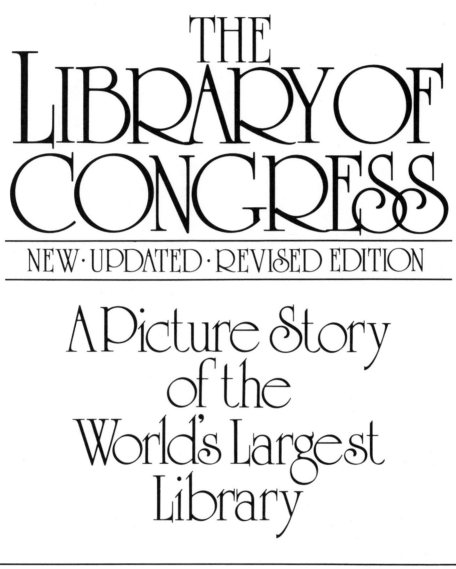

THE LIBRARY OF CONGRESS

NEW · UPDATED · REVISED EDITION

A Picture Story of the World's Largest Library

Gene Gurney & Nick Apple

with special photography by
Joseph Walters and Harold Wise

CROWN PUBLISHERS, INC.
New York

acknowledgments

The authors are indebted to Clare Gurney for preparing the 1966 edition, Joanne Apple for her extensive research for the rewrite of the book, and to Helen W. Dalrymple of the Library of Congress for the editing and proofing of the manuscript. And for the fine photography, Harold Wise, Joseph Walters, Jonathan Wallen, and James W. McClung. For other services that made the book possible, Jean Tucker, Craig L. D'ooge, and John C. Sullivan of the Library of Congress.

Inquiries should be addressed to Crown Publishers, Inc., One Park Avenue, New York, New York 10016

Printed in the United States of America

Published simultaneously in Canada by General Publishing Company Limited

Library of Congress Cataloging in Publication Data

Gurney, Gene.
  The Library of Congress.

  Includes index.
  1. Library of Congress. I. Apple, Nick P. II. Title.
Z733.U58G8 1981   027.573   81-9751
ISBN: 0-517-545179   AACR2

10 9 8 7 6 5 4 3 2 1
First Revised Edition

contents

foreword

Ours is perhaps the first nation in history to be consciously based on the literacy of its people. It is only logical and appropriate, therefore, that our national library should be a Library of Congress, a library of the people's representatives. Other great national libraries began in cabinets of curiosities, the personal treasures of monarchs and noblemen. But ours was deliberately created and calculatedly increased to enlighten the people's representatives and the people themselves.

To enter the reading rooms and consult the treasures of great national libraries of the Old World you must have letters of recommendation. Whether rooted in the slowly eroding aristocracies of history or in the arbitrary instant-elites of totalitarianism, the community of authorized readers remains restricted. Not here. Any adult can walk into our reading rooms, can consult our catalogs, can read our books. You need not prove your respectability, your political reliability—or even your literacy.

Printed books have made it possible to democratize knowledge. Books have made knowledge and ideas conveniently portable. And as books have become less expensive and more widely and more freely published,

Daniel J. Boorstin, Librarian of Congress.

The Library of Congress is not just a depository for books; it also is a museum of art. The main building in particular is commanding, its architecture imposing; and it houses a treasury of sculpture, painting, and stained glass.

LIBRARIANS OF CONGRESS

JOHN BECKLEY 1802-1807
PATRICK MAGRUDER 1807-1815
GEORGE WATTERSTON 1815-1829
JOHN SILVA MEEHAN 1829-1861
JOHN G. STEPHENSON 1861-1864
AINSWORTH RAND SPOFFORD 1864-1897

JOHN RUSSELL YOUNG 1897-1899
HERBERT PUTNAM 1899-1939
ARCHIBALD MacLEISH 1939-1944
LUTHER HARRIS EVANS 1945-1953
LAWRENCE QUINCY MUMFORD 1954-1974
DANIEL J. BOORSTIN 1975

LIBRARIAN

Left: A plaque outside the Librarian's office carries the names of the twelve men who have held the office since the Library was established by an Act of Congress in 1800. *Right:* This descriptive title is incised in marble above the door to the office of the Librarian of Congress, in the main building.

they have become interstitial and unobtrusive—a growing menace to tyrants. A growing menace, too, to all who would monopolize any kind of wealth or power, including the power of knowledge.

We must use our technology to widen the market of ideas, to increase and improve the intellectual commodity, to enlighten all consumers of knowledge. Television brings the instant present to everyone. But as Benjamin Rush warned in the early days of our Republic, we must not turn our backs on a gold mine to go chasing butterflies. We must not forget that the book, too, however venerable, is also a monument to our technology. Books bring us the durable past and the enduring present.

For most of our history, the United States has been a land of Open Gates, of new openings-up in the world. Just as our nation opened its gates to the oppressed and the persecuted of the world, so it has been a place of refuge for novel and outrageous, for obsolete and futuristic ideas. It has been a place of all sorts of openings— unimagined in other times and places. Our nation—and this Library—must remain a place of endless internal migrations of knowledge and of ideas, a catalyst and an energizer, an opener of new openings.

DANIEL J. BOORSTIN
Librarian of Congress

THE
LIBRARY OF
CONGRESS

1
ELEVEN HAIR TRUNKS AND A CASE FOR THE MAPS: 1800 GENESIS

Brigadier General Thomas Lincoln Casey, Army Chief of Engineers, directed the construction of the Library of Congress' main building from 1888 until his death in 1896. It was completed the following year, on schedule and under cost, from some 1,600 plans and drawings. This is the main entrance.

In 1789, shortly after the first Congress convened in New York City, Elbridge Gerry of Massachusetts proposed that a committee prepare a "catalog of books" for user purchase. However, his suggestion was negated by no-cost use of the New York Society Library. Note his elaborate signature.

The Library of Congress is almost as old as the United States Congress itself. Before that body moved from Philadelphia to the still uncompleted Capitol in Washington in the spring of 1800, it appropriated the sum of $5,000 "for the purchase of such books as may be necessary for the use of Congress at the said city of Washington, and for fitting up a suitable apartment for containing them." That appropriation, approved by President John Adams on April 22, 1800, marked the official beginning of the Library of Congress.

Congress, in the course of its legislative deliberations, first in New York and then in Philadelphia, had found it necessary to acquire a few standard reference works— Blackstone's *Commentaries*, Vattel's *Law of Nature and Nations*, Hume's *History of England*, Morse's *American Geography*—in all some fifty titles, plus subscriptions to a few periodicals. But in New York the members had been invited to use the 4,000-volume collection of the New York State Society Library, and in Philadelphia they had free use of the facilities of the Library Company of that city, so many more than fifty books had always been available to them. The new Federal City would offer no such library resources, however, and Congress had found it prudent to include an appropriation for a congressional library in the bill providing for the "removal and accommodation" of the government.

When, on November 22, 1800, President Adams addressed the first joint session of Congress to convene in the Senate Chamber of the new Capitol, the members had already placed a large order with the London booksellers Cadell and Davies. In December, Cadell and Davies packed 152 works in 740 volumes into eleven hair trunks for shipment to America. According to Cadell and Davies, after their arrival boxes would have been of little or no value, while trunks could readily be resold. "Two Maps of America on Canvas and Rollers" by Arrowsmith, "Charts of Chronology and Biography on Canvas and Rollers" by Priestley, and "Map of South America" by Faden were placed in a special case, and the order, except for twelve "articles not yet obtained," was on its way to Washington aboard the ship *American*.

Congress was not in session when the hair trunks and the map case arrived at the Capitol, but as soon as the Seventh Congress convened in December 1801, arrangements for the use of the new congressional library received a high priority on the legislative calendar. The room that had been occupied by the House of Representatives was set aside for library purposes. It was to be presided over by a librarian "appointed by the President of the United States solely" and paid $2 for every day of "necessary attendance." In 1802, President Thomas Jefferson chose an old friend, John James Beckley, to be the first Librarian of Congress, and Beckley, who was also the clerk of the House of Representatives, retained both jobs until his death in 1807. As Librarian of Congress he was empowered to issue books to the President, the Vice President, and members of the Senate and the House of Representatives, but three members of the House and three of the Senate, acting as a joint committee, controlled funds appropriated for the purchase of additional books for the Library.

One of the first, and wisest, things the committee did was to seek the advice of the scholarly President Jefferson, who prepared a list of books he thought should be in the Library. Prefacing his recommendations with the explanation that he had respected the committee's opinion that books of "entertainment" be excluded from the Library and that books in other languages "are not to be admitted freely" and that he had included only "those branches of science which belong to the deliberations of the members as statesmen," Jefferson listed histories that emphasized facts and dates; a wide selection of books on the law of nature and nations, "a branch of science often under discussion in Congress"; two encyclopedias; dictionaries in the languages he felt would be needed most; and a number of reference books on general law subjects. Until 1806, all purchases for the Library of Congress were made in Europe, and the committee sent the President's list to London for procurement.

The book collection of the Library of Congress grew as booksellers filled its orders and public-spirited citizens donated material, among them Secretary of State James Madison, who gave the Library two copies of the *Leyden Gazette* for the year 1807. Among the authors donating books was Mrs. Mercy Warren of Plymouth, Massachusetts, who gave her three-volume work *History of the Rise, Progress and Termination of the American Revolution Interspersed with Biographical, Political and Moral Observations.*

By 1814, the Library, then located in a small committee room, had accumulated 3,000 volumes. On August 24 of that year most of them were lost when British forces captured Washington and burned the Capitol, using books from the Library as kindling. Indignation was widespread at such wanton destruction, and Congress quickly appropriated funds to repair the damage and to purchase books and maps to replace those that

This facsimile of an 1802 catalog shows an early method of classification. Computers perform a similar function today at the Library. A folio (*top of second column*) is a book with pages printed on pieces of paper cut two from a sheet; a quarto is a book with pages cut four from a sheet.

Above: Thomas Jefferson often is referred to as the "father" of the Library of Congress. When his collection of 6,487 volumes was added to the Library in 1815, the Library was transformed from a special library to a general library. President Jefferson also appointed the first two Librarians, John James Beckley and Patrick Magruder. *Right:* These books and documents were among those that President Jefferson sold to the Library and are now part of the Rare Book and Special Collections Division.

had been destroyed. Thomas Jefferson, retired from the presidency and living at Monticello but still interested in the Library of Congress, offered his personal book collection, which he estimated at "between nine and ten thousand volumes" and containing everything, he declared, "chiefly valuable in science and literature." He wrote: "I do not know that it contains any branch of science which Congress would wish to exclude from their collection; there is, in fact, no subject to which a Member of Congress may not have occasion to refer."

Jefferson had always hoped that after his death Congress would purchase his personal library. The shameful burning of the Capitol, coupled with his own pressing need for money, prompted him to make an immediate offer. He suggested an appraisal to determine the value of his collection; one was made, and early in 1815, his library of 6,487 volumes became the property of the United States government for the sum of $23,950. That purchase not only reestablished the Library of Congress but also more than doubled its size and, most important of all, changed its character from a special library to a general library.

Jefferson's books were delivered in long pine boxes to the building on E Street called Blodget's Hotel, where Congress met temporarily during the rebuilding of the Capitol. There they were placed in a library room presided over by George Watterston, the first full-time Librarian of Congress. After spending almost $24,000 for books, Congress had decided that its Library needed more care than the clerk of the House of Representatives could give it. Under Watterston's direction the books received bookplates and labels, but they remained in the arrangement that Jefferson had devised, an adaptation of

Bacon's classification of science according to the faculties of mind employed—memory, reason, or imagination, with forty-four subdivisions.

Patrons of the Library of Congress in Blodget's Hotel described it as "very beautiful" and winning "the approbation of all"; however, in 1818, the books were moved to much less desirable temporary quarters in the attic of the Capitol. Restoration of the building was still under way, and the crowded attic rooms lacked adequate shelving, making it necessary for books to be stacked on the tables; but the Library remained there until 1824, when it moved again—this time downstairs to the newly finished "Library hall," considered by many to be the most beautiful room, not only in the Capitol but in the entire city of Washington. The Library had occupied its fine new quarters only briefly when, on the night of December 22, 1825, Congressman Edward Everett, returning to his home near the Capitol, observed a flickering light that seemed to come from the Library. He alerted a Capitol guard, who looked through the keyhole of the locked Library door and reported that everything appeared to be in order. When the guard returned to the door later in the evening, there were definite signs of a fire inside. Librarian Watterston, hastily summoned from his home, unlocked the door to discover a fire in one of the galleries. The blaze was small, but no buckets could be found to carry water from a pump on the other side of the building. While a bell in the Capitol yard sounded an alarm, guards ran through the adjacent streets awakening the householders, who turned out to fight the fire. In spite of the delay, damage to the Library was limited.

Unfortunately, that was not the case on December 24, 1851, when another fire broke out in the Library. Caused by an overheated flue, that fire engulfed the main reading room and spread to the roof and dome before it could be controlled by Washington firemen. The Library of Congress lost almost 35,000 books, including half of the original Jefferson collection, and for months while repairs were under way, operated from what had been its document room and a portion of the adjoining passage.

The Library of Congress moved into an elaborate fireproof Library Room in the late summer of 1852. Volumes damaged by fire, water, or rough handling had been repaired, and new books had been purchased to replace those destroyed by the fire. In addition, a large number of donations had been received, making it possible for the Library to reopen with 25,000 volumes on its shelves. It continued to grow at a rapid rate. Some years earlier Congress had agreed to let the Library

George Watterston was the first full-time Librarian of Congress, serving from 1815 to 1829. For several years during his term, the Library was located in Blodget's Hotel on E Street.

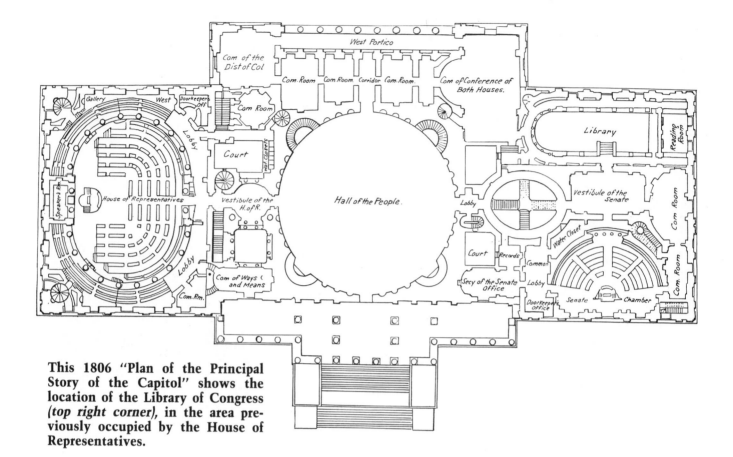

This 1806 "Plan of the Principal Story of the Capitol" shows the location of the Library of Congress *(top right corner)*, in the area previously occupied by the House of Representatives.

exchange government documents and duplicate books with foreign libraries. Such exchanges brought in not only additional material but also material that widened the scope of the collections, as did a law passed in 1846 requiring that one copy of every article registered for copyright be deposited in the Library.

As the Library grew in size and scope, its influence spread. The privilege of borrowing books was extended to the members of the President's Cabinet, the secretary of the Senate, the clerk of the House of Representatives, the congressional chaplains, and "any individual, when in the District of Columbia, who may have been President of the United States." In addition, visitors were admitted to the Library and allowed to consult the books there, since Congress, while retaining complete control of the management of the Library, recognized that its contents could serve the entire government and provide a limited reference service to the public as well.

On December 31, 1864, in the last year of the Civil War, President Lincoln appointed Ainsworth Rand Spofford as Librarian of Congress. Under his guidance during the next thirty-two years, the Library expanded its services to Congress and to the entire nation. A

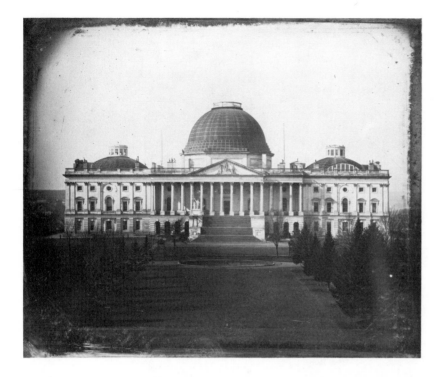

When this daguerreotype was made, around 1846, the Library was still located in the right rear portion of the Capitol. The Senate and House wings, and a new dome, were added later. This photograph, attributed to John Plumbe, Jr., is from the Library's Prints and Photographs Division.

bookseller and publisher turned journalist, Spofford had been named First Assistant Librarian of Congress in 1861, and his performance in that position won him the support of several members of the Joint Committee on the Library when the incumbent Librarian, Dr. John G. Stephenson, who followed John S. Meehan, fourth Librarian, resigned in 1864.

Spofford's appointment coincided with a renewal of legislative interest in the Library. Early in 1865, Congress appropriated $160,000 to add some badly needed space and strengthened the copyright law by revoking protection unless a copy of a book, pamphlet, map, chart, musical composition, print, engraving, or photograph was sent "free of postage" to the Library of Congress. These deposits produced many valuable additions to the collections and greatly enhanced the Library's status as a national institution. As a result of exchanges, the copyright deposits (increased to two copies of each work in 1870), and the transfer of the library of the Smithsonian Institution, the number of volumes in the Library of Congress increased from 82,000 to 237,000 between 1865 and 1870. By judicious use of this material and by concentrating purchases on rare items and volumes that would round out the collections, Librarian Spofford ensured the development of a great national library for the United States.

In spite of the additional space acquired in 1865, the Library's quarters in the Capitol were soon filled to

Following the disastrous fire, the section of the Capitol occupied by the Library was rebuilt with ceilings, floorplates, bookshelves, and balcony railings made of iron.

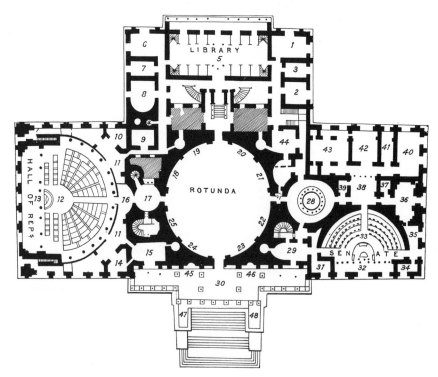

An elaborate fireproof Iron Room, constructed in a space west of the Rotunda after the 1851 fire that destroyed nearly 35,000 volumes, served as the Library until 1897.

This drawing, made by James Wilson Bengough for *Harper's Weekly*, shows how crowded the Library had become by 1897. The figure at the right is the sixth Librarian, Ainsworth Rand Spofford.

overflowing. In his annual report for 1872, Spofford complained: "There is no possible place for the arrangement or filing of the current periodicals, many of which, therefore, remain comparatively useless for reference until they are bound." He continued: "Masses of books, pamphlets, newspapers, engravings, etc., in the course of collation, cataloguing, labeling, and stamping, in preparation for their proper location in the Library, are necessarily always under the eye and almost under the feet of members of Congress and other visitors."

Although Spofford was accused of deliberately piling up books and other material to impress congressmen with the need for more space, the Library had in fact outgrown its suite of rooms west of the rotunda and overflowed into nooks and corners of the Capitol where there was no fire protection. Spofford, unable to find existing space in the Capitol that would accommodate his rapidly growing library for more than a few years, strongly recommended a separate building designed especially for library purposes or, failing that, an extension of the Capitol's west front to create more space.

In spite of the obviously crowded condition of the Library, it was fifteen years before Congress appropriated money for a new building and eleven more before

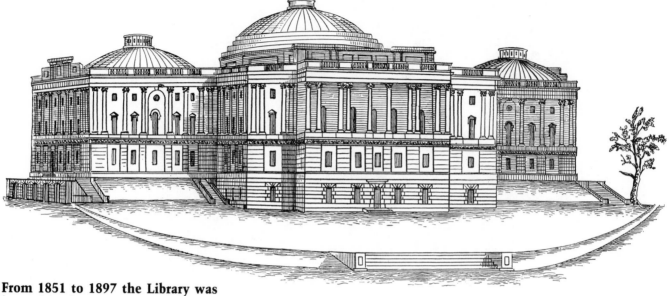

From 1851 to 1897 the Library was housed in the center rear portion of the Capitol, facing what is now the National Mall.

construction was completed. In the meantime Spofford and his staff carried on the work of the Library as best they could. They issued annual reports, a yearly catalog of acquisitions until 1872, and a catalog covering the years 1873 to 1875. In 1869, a two-volume work, *The Catalogue of the Library of Congress: Index of Subjects*, appeared. It was a monumental listing, alphabetically by subject, of all the books in the Library. Spofford strongly favored such alphabetical arrangements, even though several large American libraries had developed more sophisticated classification schemes. He also failed to adopt the printed catalog cards already in use in some libraries, although the Library of Congress did develop an author catalog on large cards, with entries in part clipped from printed catalogs. In Spofford's opinion, the Library of Congress lacked both the space and the staff for ambitious classification and cataloging projects. Today, an overall evaluation of Spofford's contribution indicates that he was one of the great Librarians of Congress.

In 1886, Congress finally appropriated $500,000 to start the construction of a new Library building immediately to the east of the Capitol. When, more than a decade later, the time came for the Library of Congress to vacate its crowded rooms in the Capitol, there had to be moved nearly 750,000 books; 18,000 volumes of newspapers and a great many magazines, bound and unbound; 200,000 musical scores and songs; an esti-

The Library's cornerstone, laid in 1890, contains the annual reports of the Librarian of Congress for 1872 and 1888, the annual reports of the Army's Chief of Engineers for 1869 and 1888, a photograph of an architect's drawing of the southwest elevation of the building, a photograph of the construction site as it appeared in August 1890, and synopses of legislative reports and directives relating to the construction of the building.

When this picture was taken in 1893, the Library, under construction since 1889, was still four years from completion.

mated 250,000 engravings, etchings, photographs, and similar pieces; more than 40,000 charts and maps; and numerous valuable manuscripts. The transfer to the new building took place during the summer and fall of 1897. Workers placed books and other materials in handbarrows and open trays of pine, each of which held the contents of a shelf, and carried them to a horse-drawn wagon for the trip from the Capitol across the

American artists supplied most of
the decorative work for the new
Library of Congress building in the
late nineteenth century. Here, marble cutters and other artisans work
on material for friezes and ornamen-
tation.

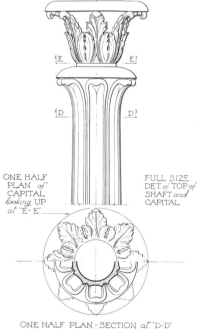

ONE HALF
PLAN of
CAPITAL
looking UP
at 'E-E'

FULL SIZE
DET of TOP of
SHAFT and
CAPITAL

ONE HALF PLAN - SECTION at 'D-D'
FULL SIZE DETAIL

TYPICAL BRONZE LIGHTING STANDARD for
LIBRARY of CONGRESS MAIN BLDG. GROUNDS

East Plaza and grounds to the new Library of Congress,
where other workmen carried the trays and barrows to
the places where the materials were to be placed on
shelves or stored. During the transfer great care was
taken to keep the books in exact order, even though they
had to be "brushed and beaten to free them from dust."

Books and other materials were removed from eigh-
teen places in the Capitol in addition to the three rooms
and four storerooms formally assigned to the Library.
Even the area in the subbasement that housed the
Capitol gas meters stored copyright deposits, unbound
periodicals, and documents. When the move was completed in November 1897, it was estimated that the
Library of Congress, once contained in eleven hair
trunks and a case for the maps, had grown until the
weight of its holdings totaled 1,000 tons.

William de Leftwich Dodge painted the subjects of Literature, Music, Science, Art, and Ambition in the northwest pavilion. Like many artisans at the time, he wore a coat and tie under his work smock.

First Street and the new Library of Congress appeared like this in 1897, when the collection was transferred by handbarrows and wagons from the Capitol. The toga-draped statue of George Washington now is located in the Smithsonian's National Museum of American History. Blemishes in the photograph are from the original.

2
A GREAT NATIONAL LIBRARY: NEW HOME

Gleaming white Italian marble and twin staircases are the major attractions of the Main Entrance Hall to the Library. Temporary office partitions off the gallery level were removed in 1980 when the Madison Building was occupied, thus revealing much of the previously hidden beauty.

The Library of Congress began operations in its own building under the direction of a new Librarian. On June 30, 1897, President William McKinley appointed John Russell Young, a journalist and diplomat, to the post. Young, in turn, asked the veteran Ainsworth Spofford to stay on as his chief assistant, and together they organized for expanded services in the new building following the general plan outlined by Congress in the Library appropriations bill passed early in 1897. The Library reopened with a reading room, a copyright office, an art gallery, a hall of maps, a periodical department, a music department, a manuscript department, a law library, a catalog department, and a section charged with the supervision of the building and grounds.

Librarian Young gave his active support to several projects, including the further development of the collections, books for the blind, and the extension of the hours during which the reading room was open to the public, but his term of office was cut short by his death early in 1899. Under his successor, Herbert Putnam, Librarian of the Boston Public Library prior to his appointment to the Library of Congress in March 1899, the Library became one of the world's great national libraries.

Putnam was a professional librarian with definite ideas about the part the Library of Congress should play in the life of the nation. In 1896, representing the American Library Association before the Joint Committee on the Library, he declared: "This should be a library . . . which stands foremost as a model and example of assisting forward the work of scholarship in the United States." Putnam strongly recommended enlarging the scope, function, and equipment of the Library and making its contents more available to the public through the development of an efficient classification and cataloging system. During his forty years as Librarian of Congress he did all that and more.

When Putnam took over the administration of the Library, large numbers of books and other materials awaited processing in all the departments. The classification system then in use was basically the same one Thomas Jefferson developed for his library. While it had worked well in a private library, it was inadequate for the large, rapidly growing Library of Congress, and staff shortages had added to the cataloging problem. The new Librarian proposed to reclassify the entire collection, rearrange the books and pamphlets according to the new system, and set up a dictionary card catalog for the use of the public. The results were the development of the

A pen-and-ink drawing of the Library of Congress from an early postcard. Note the horse-drawn buggy in front of the steps and the fountain.

Library of Congress classification system and the reclassification of a million books and pamphlets.

The cards made by Library of Congress catalogers for reclassified material, for previously uncataloged material, and for additions to the Library were printed, and extra cards were sold to anyone who wanted them—a service of great value to the libraries of the United States. Another important nationwide service inaugurated by Putnam was a supplemental loan system that made it possible for libraries to borrow material from the Library of Congress for the use of serious researchers in their local communities. In still another extension of service, designated university and public libraries received complete sets of Library of Congress cards, a move that promoted uniformity and accuracy in cataloging, enabled the depository libraries and libraries in their vicinities to order cards by number, and provided researchers throughout the country with information about books available in the Library of Congress. Service to researchers was further extended in 1927, when a Rockefeller grant enabled the Library of Congress to set up the National Union Catalog to record the important books available in the United States on every subject and in the libraries where they are located.

While its services were being extended to the far corners of the United States, the holdings of the Library of Congress grew in every field of knowledge. Government departments and bureaus were instructed to give excess documents of a useful nature to the Librarian, individual citizens presented important printed and pictorial materials, and foreign publications were acquired in increasing numbers. The Library of Congress gained wide acceptance as one of the best libraries in the world, but once again lack of space became a serious problem. Over the years extra bookstacks had been erected wherever there was room; it had even become necessary to store books in the cellars. Relief came in 1939 with the opening of the five-story Annex east of the main building and connected to it by a tunnel running under Second Street S.E. The Annex, renamed the Thomas Jefferson Building in 1976, provided shelf space for 10 million books in its central core beneath the fifth floor. (Both buildings would be renamed in 1980.) But by 1959 more space was needed again as the Library continued to grow under Putnam's successors: Archibald MacLeish (1939–1944), Luther Evans (1945–1953), L. Quincy Mumford (1954–1974), and Daniel J. Boorstin (since 1975).

Once again books and staff members were crowded into cellars and into areas intended for exhibition halls. As early as 1956, Mumford and the architect of the Capitol began to discuss the need for more space. The most succinct expression of the Library's problem was made two years later when Mumford told the Joint Committee of Congress, "We have reached the place where we are literally bursting at the seams." At the time the Library was growing at the rate of one new item each second. Accordingly, in May 1960, Congress directed the architect of the Capitol to prepare plans for an additional building for the Library. At nearly the same time Congress also established a committee to plan a memorial to James Madison. Eventually, in October 1965, Congress authorized $75 million for the construction of the Library of Congress James Madison Memorial Building directly south of the main Library building. Ground was broken in June 1971 and occupancy began in early 1980, after $123 million had been appropriated for the nine-story building, two stories of which are completely underground. Historians recall the appropriateness of linking the memorial with the Library, in that Madison had proposed as early as 1783 that a collection of books for "a library for Congress" be assembled. And his achievements in the realm of ideas make a major library building a fitting memorial.

In June 1980, the other two buildings received new names. Public Law 96–269, approved by President Jimmy Carter on June 13, renamed the main Library of Congress Building as the Library of Congress Thomas Jefferson Building. The original Thomas Jefferson Building (formerly the Annex) became the Library of Congress John Adams Building. Thus, the three-building Library of Congress complex is now named after the first three Presidents who resided in Washington and who were involved in the establishment of the Library. The name change resulted from a plan of the architect of the Capitol to have a uniform sign system for Capitol Hill buildings.

With the occupancy of the Madison Building that same year, plans were under way to restore the Library's two other buildings to their intended uses. As the partitions and temporary office walls in the Jefferson Building come down, this building's beautiful exhibit areas and ornate interior features will be restored to their original splendor. The Adams Building will return to its original annex function, that of an efficiently organized storehouse of books.

When MacLeish became Librarian in 1939, he found the whole of the Library of Congress "suspended like a

Granite from Troy, New Hampshire, was used in the construction of the impressive stairways leading to the west or main entrance of the Library. Many distinguished guests are welcomed on the central landing, which is laid with flagstones of red Missouri granite. Republic of China Ambassador Chow Shu-kai is being greeted in 1969 by Librarian L. Quincy Mumford.

Sculptor Roland Hinton Perry designed "The Court of Neptune," the elaborate fountain that decorates the approach to the Library of Congress. It features a bronze figure of Neptune flanked by nymphs riding sea horses. Jets and splashing water add a sense of action in the close-up of the sea-nymph and horse.

A close-up of Neptune.

From the central landing, a grand staircase continues to the entrance of the main building. Note the sculptured head above the window to the right of the lamppost.

Thirty-three sculptured heads illustrating the races of mankind decorate the main building's first-story windows. This head represents the brunette European type.

wasp's nest" from the Office of the Librarian and decided that his first task would be the reorganization of this antiquated and inefficient structure. The organization that he planned, decentralizing the administration of the Library, endured through a period of unparalleled growth, through a major war and the information explosion that followed. When Boorstin became Librarian in 1975, he found the Library still operating essentially as it had in the 1940s. He appointed a Task Force on Goals, Organization, and Planning that was to recommend, after sufficient study, the changes that were needed in the Library of the 1980s and beyond. The task force, a staff group aided by advisory committees representing various Library constituencies, made its report in January 1977, and a Planning Office was established to implement its recommendations. In 1978, there was a major reorganization of the Library of Congress, the first in thirty-five years.

Like that of MacLeish, the Boorstin plan decentralized, leaving policy direction, with the concurrence of the Congressional Joint Committee on the Library, in the hands of the Librarian, Deputy Librarian, Associate Librarian, and Associate Librarians for Management and for National Programs. The Associate Librarians for Management and National Programs share responsibility for directing the day-to-day operations of the Library with three Assistant Librarians, the Director

Arabian.

Blond European.

Circassian.

Hungarian.

Persian.

Hindu.

of the Congressional Research Service, and the Law Librarian. These officers head the seven departments of the Library: Management, National Programs, Research Services, Processing Services, Copyright Office, Law Library, and Congressional Research Service.

The Associate Librarian for Management is in charge

of finance, personnel, automation, photoduplication, and three other divisions and offices that provide support services to the whole of the Library. The Associate Librarian for National Programs directs programs that can be characterized as outreach activities: exhibits, publishing, and information, service to the blind and physically handicapped, children's literature, educational liaison, and the American Folklife Center. Two of these programs were renamed to indicate their status more clearly: the National Library Service for the Blind and Physically Handicapped, and the Children's Literature Center.

The Reader Services and Research departments were united in the Research Services department. Three directors report to the Assistant Librarian for Research Services: the Director for Area Studies, whose present responsibilities include the European, Asian, Hispanic, and African and Middle Eastern Divisions; the Director for General Reference, who is responsible for reading rooms, collection management, loans, serials, and science and technology; and the Director for Special Collections, who manages music, prints and photographs, manuscripts, rare books, and maps functions, as well as materials services in the new Motion Picture, Broadcasting, and Recorded Sound Division.

The Assistant Librarian for Processing Services directs all technical processing activities of the Library through three directors—for Acquisitions and Overseas Operations, for Cataloging, and for Processing Systems, Networks, and Automatic Planning. The Register of Copyrights, who also holds the title of Assistant Librarian for Copyright Services, heads a department, the Copyright Office, which in 1978 was extensively reorganized and strengthened to carry out the new copyright legislation enacted in 1976.

Another activity in the Library of Congress was the result of the review of the Library undertaken by Boorstin's task force. Two of the advisory groups that worked with the task force, those representing librarians and publishers, urged the Library to play a more prominent educational role in the national culture and especially in enhancing appreciation of the book and the printed word. In Public Law 95–129, signed by the President on October 13, 1977, Congress created the Center for the Book in the Library of Congress and affirmed its agreement with the task force recommendation, stating its belief in "the importance of the printed word and the book" and recognizing the need for continued study and development of the written record as "central to our understanding of ourselves and our world."

Bela L. Pratt modeled the six spandrel figures of the main entrance porch. The pairs represent *(left to right)* Literature, Science, and Art. One figure *(second from right)* holds a mallet in her left hand while studying a bust of Dante.

The center was created to "provide a program for the investigation of the transmission of human knowledge and to heighten public interest in the role of books and printing in the diffusion of knowledge." This purpose was to be accomplished through such activities as "a visiting scholar program accompanied by lectures, exhibits, publications, and any other related activities." In carrying out the center's functions, the Librarian of Congress was authorized to receive money and other gifts and to accept and use the services of voluntary help.

At the end of 1980 the holdings of the Library of Congress numbered 76,945,360 items, of which 19,155,165 were books and pamphlets. To maintain these collections and to carry out the Library's responsibilities to the Congress and to the public, Congress appropriated $179,517,000. This amount includes $6.5 million received for sales by the Cataloging Distribution Service and $4.6 million received in fees by the Copyright Office.

Although this marble eagle overlooking the main entrance area is historically American, the Jefferson Building is in the style of the Italian Renaissance.

A bust of Dante *(right)* is one of nine portrait busts of famous writers that stand before circular windows at the second-floor level of the main building. The busts are the work of sculptors J. Scott Hartley, Herbert Adams, and F. Wellington Ruckstuhl. The others commemorated with Dante in the portico are Demosthenes, Emerson, Irving, Goethe, Franklin, Macaulay, Hawthorne, and Scott *(shown above)*. Wiring is used to discourage birds.

Above left: **Massive, ornate bronze doors—measuring fourteen feet to the top of the arch—protect the three deep arches of the entrance porch. The door symbolizing Tradition *(left)* was modeled by Olin L. Warner, and like the others, it weighs more than one ton. *Above:* The center doors, by Frederick MacMonnies, symbolize the Art of Printing, with the two women holding torches representing the Humanities *(left)* and Intellect. *Left:* Writing is the subject of the right set of doors leading to the first floor of the Jefferson Building. Herbert Adams completed these doors after Warner's death in 1896.**

A section of the stained-glass panels in the ceiling seems like an elaborate spider's web.

At each corner of a skylight high above the great hall, female half-figures flank cartouches containing a lamp and a book, the symbols of learning.

"Oral Traditions" depicts an Arabian story-teller relating his marvelous tales to a circle of listeners.

The east arcade of the Great Hall contains six colorful panels by John W. Alexander illustrating the evolution of the book. In the first panel, "The Cairn," primitive men clad in skins are shown piling stones, perhaps as a memorial or record of some event.

A young Egyptian cuts an inscription on a temple in "Hieroglyphics" while his girl watches.

"Pictograph" shows an American Indian drawing a story on an animal skin.

A monk working on a parchment is the subject of "The Manuscript Book."

The sixth and last panel in the evolution of the book, "The Printing Press," depicts Gutenberg examining a printed page.

Ceilings of corridors in the main building also are elaborately decorated and represent fields of knowledge.

Semielliptical paintings by H. O. Walker occupy the space within the arches at the east end of the Main Entrance Hall's south corridor. His principal mural, "Lyric Poetry," suggests the inspiration of poetry through the representations of *(left to right)* Mirth—the only male—Beauty, Passion, Lyric Poetry, Pathos, Truth, and Devotion. In six accompanying murals, Walker honors noted poets.

Comus, the vile enchanter, is Walker's selection to illustrate the poetry of John Milton.

Endymion, in John Keats' poem of that name, sleeps on Mount Latmos, while his lover Diana, the moon, shines down upon him.

"Palace of Art," for Alfred Lord Tennyson, shows Ganymede upon the back of an eagle, which represents Jupiter.

"Boy of Winander" is based on William Wordsworth's poem beginning "There was a Boy."

"Adonis," from *Venus and Adonis* by William Shakespeare, depicts the youth's death.

Forty-eight stars representing the states and territories of the United States in 1896 surround the great seal of the nation in this overhead painting by Elmer E. Garnsey. The four lyres represent the fine arts.

Portions of the mosaic ceiling in the hall outside the Main Reading Room honor Law and Theology.

This mosaic entitled "Law," executed in Venice by Frederick Dielman, is in the original reading room for members of the House of Representatives.

Like most of the special mural decorations in the main building, Charles Sprague Pearce's were painted in oils on canvas, then affixed to the wall with a composition of white lead. Shown are "Religion" and "Labor," part of "The Family" series.

The "Greek Heroes" collection was painted by Walter McEwen. Paris is shown on the left conversing with Menelaus and his wife, Helen of Troy.

Melpomene, the Muse of Tragedy, has the tragic mask at her right foot. Edward Simmons did this and eight other Greek mythological goddesses. Melpomene is flanked by two genii, one holding a laurel crown and the other a brazier of fire.

Cherubic figures representing *(from left)* Comedy, Poetry, and Tragedy adorn the top landing of the main building's south staircase.

A Christmas tree seventy-five feet high would fit in the Main Entrance Hall. Carolers line the grand marble staircase and edges of the mosaic marble floor. The white marble is from Italy and the brown from Tennessee.

The second floor in the Main Entrance Hall has been called the Hall of Columns.

One of two marble staircases in the main hall. The bronze figure was designed and executed by Philip Martiny and rises ten feet above its newel post.

Like the rest of the main building, the vaulted ceilings of the second floor are lavishly decorated.

This mark of a sixteenth-century French printer is one of fifty-six such printers' and publishers' marks, painted on the ceilings, from England, Scotland, the United States, Italy, Spain, Belgium, Germany, and France.

The mosaic mural on the landing, "The Minerva of Peace" by Elihu Vedder, took seven years to complete and measures fifteen feet six inches high. The stairs lead from the second floor of the main building to the gallery area above.

Holding her two-headed spear, the Minerva of Peace never relaxes her vigil against the enemies of the country she protects.

The famous Main Reading Room of the Library of Congress opened its doors to the public on November 1, 1897. The first book issued, Martha Lamb's *History of the City of New York*, went to an employee of the Department of Agriculture. Sixteen bronze statues overlook the area from the gallery. They range from Michelangelo to William Shakespeare.

From the elaborate Great Hall of the Library of Congress, the door in the center background leads to the Main Reading Room.

LIBRARY OF CONGRESS

ERECTED UNDER THE ACTS OF CONGRESS OF
APRIL 15 1886 OCTOBER 2 1888 AND MARCH 2 1889 BY
BRIG. GEN. THOS. LINCOLN CASEY
CHIEF OF ENGINEERS U.S.A.

BERNARD R. GREEN SUPT. AND ENGINEER
JOHN L. SMITHMEYER ARCHITECT
PAUL J. PELZ ARCHITECT
EDWARD PEARCE CASEY ARCHITECT

Government is the central figure in this painting above the door to the Main Reading Room. The youth to her right holds a bridle representing the restraining influence of Order, while the other youth holds the sword of Defense and Justice.

Frederick MacMonnies' bronze statue of Shakespeare gazes as if deep in thought. The head is a composite of the portrait in the first collected editions of the *Plays* and the Stratford bust.

From the gallery visitors can view the Main Reading Room two levels below. The statue in the foreground is that of Sir Isaac Newton by C. E. Dallin.

The statues of Ludwig van Beethoven *(left)* and Sir Francis Bacon *(right)* illustrate the detail found in the sixteen portrait statues.

Details of the wall decorations behind the bronze statues can be seen in this segment of the gallery.

This representation of Philosophy by Bela L. Pratt is one of eight plaster statues symbolizing fields of human endeavor. The other seven, also located above the gallery, represent Art, Commerce, History, Law, Poetry, Religion, and Science. Bacon's inscription at the top reads: "The inquiry, knowledge, and belief of truth is the sovereign good of human nature."

"Commerce" by John Flanagan.

Female figures dominate the frieze above the plaster statues and decorative windows.

"Art" by Francois M. L. Tonetti-Dozzi.

Eight semicircular stained-glass windows contain seals of the original forty-eight states. Each window also features the great seal of the United States topped by the American eagle.

This is the massive dome above the Main Reading Room as seen from the gallery of bronze statues. The collar mural actually forms a part of the painting in the higher dome.

Inside the very top of
the Rotunda dome.

The function of a great library is to preserve the records of the
"Evolution of Civilization," the title of this dome painting by
Edwin Howland Blashfield. In the center is a female figure lifting a
veil from her eyes, thus symbolizing intellectual progress—starting
with ancient Egypt *(top left)* and progressing to modern America
(top right).

A life-size Father Time dominates the Library's great clock below the visitors' gallery in the Rotunda. Sculptor John Flanagan also included four bronze maidens to represent the seasons.

After being closed for nearly a year, the Main Reading Room reopened in August 1965 with a new floor, a new lighting, heating, and ventilating system, and a new book-carrier system. The Library's great clock is above the screened walkway *(right)*.

The Woodrow Wilson Room is the locale for the signing of the official guest book by King Mahendra of Nepal in 1960. Queen Ratna and Librarian L. Quincy Mumford watch.

Workmen periodically clean mosaic and other decorative works to maintain their full beauty. The inscription from Wordsworth *(bottom center)* reads: "The poets who on Earth have made us heirs of truth and pure delight by heavenly lays."

A view of the dome after scaffolding had been erected during the cleaning and restoration of the Main Reading Room.

Chief executives confer in the Deputy Librarian's office, located in the Jefferson Building.

An Air Corps photographer snapped this view in the late 1930s as the Library's Annex *(bottom left)* was nearing completion. The Folger Shakespeare Library is to the right of the Annex (now the Adams Building) and the Supreme Court is to the right of the main Library building. The Madison Building was constructed during the 1970s to the left of the main building. The National Mall extends westerly from the Capitol. *U.S. Air Force Photo*

Tourists on the front steps of the U.S. Capitol have this view of the Library's Jefferson Building.

Although separated by a long city block, the current dome of the Capitol appears to hover directly alongside the Jefferson Building. The optical illusion was achieved through the use of a telephoto lens.

Representatives in the Cannon House Office Building have this view of the 1897 Jefferson Building and the 1939 Adams Building.

The Jefferson Building as seen from the main entrance of the Madison Building.

South side of the Adams Building as seen from Third Street and Independence Avenue.

By 1939, when the Library of Congress Annex was completed, library architecture had become less ornate. The Annex was later named in honor of President Thomas Jefferson and then in 1980 was renamed in honor of President John Adams. At the same time, the main Library building was named in honor of Jefferson.

Elaborate bronze doors guard the principal entrance to the Adams Building. The three sets of double doors at the east and west entrances are decorated with bas-relief sculptures designed by Lee Lawrie. Shown here are the center doors at the west entrance with figures of Hermes, Odin, Ogma, Itzamna, Quetzalcoatl, and Sequoyah—all of whom are credited with giving the art of writing to their people. The same design is repeated on the north and south doors at the east entrance.

More leaders who gave writing to their people are depicted on the center doors at the east entrance. They are Thoth, Ts'ang Chieh, Nabu, Brahma, Cadmus, and Tamurath. This design is repeated in the two flanking doorways at the west entrance.

A single bronze doorway at the south entrance to the Adams Building features relatively modern people. The male figure symbolizes physical labor and the female intellectual labor.

Entrances to the Adams Building are decorated with stone sculptures executed in bas-relief.

THE GROUND OF LIBERTY IS TO BE GAINED BY INCHES · WE MUST BE CONTENTED TO SECURE WHAT WE CAN GET FROM TIME TO TIME AND ETERNALLY PRESS FORWARD FOR WHAT IS YET TO GET · IT TAKES TIME TO PERSUADE MEN TO DO EVEN WHAT IS FOR THEIR OWN GOOD.

THOSE WHO LABOR IN THE EARTH ARE THE CHOSEN PEOPLE OF GOD IF HE EVER HAD A CHOSEN PEOPLE WHOSE BREASTS HE HAS MADE THE PECULIAR DEPOSITS FOR SUBSTANTIAL AND GENUINE VIRTUE · IT IS THE FOCUS IN WHICH HE KEEPS ALIVE THAT SACRED FIRE WHICH OTHERWISE MIGHT ESCAPE FROM THE EARTH.

Panels in the Jefferson mural illustrate his writings on Freedom, Labor, Education, and Democratic Government.

The Adams Building reflects the style and economy of the Depression era.

While it is not as elaborately decorated as the main building, the Adams Building does contain works of art. This is its Main Reading Room with the famous Thomas Jefferson murals by Ezra Winter in the upper panels.

"The Library of Congress James Madison Memorial Building" is the official title of the latest addition to the Library complex along Independence Avenue *(right)*. In the right background is the Cannon House Office Building.

President James Madison in 1783 proposed "a library for Congress." In August 1978, sculptor Walker Hancock supervised the placement of the Madison statue in the new nine-story building named in Madison's honor.

The 1981 annual exhibit of the White House News Photographers Association was the first held in the new Madison Building.

3
INFORMATION FOR THE NATION: RESEARCH SERVICES

Bound volumes also are studied in the Newspaper and Current Periodical Reading Room.

Providing the vast amount of information needed by government agencies, industry, scholars, and ordinary citizens in today's rapidly changing world is the responsibility of the Research Services department of the Library of Congress. The largest of the Library's departments, it administers both general and specialized collections and serves those who write or telephone for information as well as those who visit the library in person, *if* the information is not available in the inquirer's local state library. The Research Services' staff of subject specialists and librarians prepares bibliographies and other aids to research for publication and for the use of government agencies, recommends material to be purchased for the Library's collections and material to be retained from the more than 9 million pieces received each year through exchanges with libraries in the United States and abroad, gifts, copyright deposits, and transfer from other government agencies.

Research Services is divided into three primary sections supervised by directors for Area Studies, General Reference, and Special Collections. Under the Director for Area Studies are the African and Middle Eastern, Asian, European, and Hispanic divisions. An American Division will be created when adequate funds are available. Six divisions are under the Director for General Reference: Collections Management, Federal Research, General Reading Rooms, Loan, Science and Technology, and Serial and Government Publications. Special Collections includes the Geography and Map; Manuscript; Motion Picture, Broadcasting and Recorded Sound; Music; Prints and Photographs; and Rare Book and Special Collections divisions. These titles serve as an indication of the breadth of assistance offered the general public through Research Services, which also includes a National Referral Center and a Preservation Office. A sampling of the department's services follows.

The Library receives over 1,600 newspapers, two-thirds of them foreign publications.

SIXTEEN HUNDRED NEWSPAPERS

The Library of Congress receives and makes available for reference 550 United States newspapers and 1,120 newspapers published in foreign countries. Its back-dated newspapers are preserved in 70,500 bound volumes and 368,000 reels of microfilm. The Library's extensive Serial Division collections, which include magazines and other periodical publications as well as newspapers, have been consulted by as many as 75,000 persons in one year, with another 1,000 persons receiving information by mail and 14,000 by telephone.

Copies of the *Times* of London are available on microfilm, as are copies of the *New York Times* and others.

Microfilm readers such as these are used extensively for researching back-dated newspapers in the Serial Division's Periodical Room.

Note-taking can be facilitated greatly through the use of microfilm printers, which quickly produce negative copies as shown here.

Assistance is provided at the reference desk.

THE NATION'S LITERARY TREASURES

All of the half million items in this division are available for study by scholars.

A book becomes "rare" when it is one of the first of its kind or when it is closely associated with a famous person or event; or it may be a very scarce and valuable item. The Library of Congress has acquired more than 500,000 books, pamphlets, broadsides, and related objects for the collections of its Rare Book and Special Collections Division, and all of them are available for study by scholars.

Over one third of the volumes in the division's collections are shelved in one continuous arrangement by Library of Congress classification. This portion of the collection contains at least a few books in virtually every subject that the Library collects. Although the materials the division houses have come into its custody for a variety of reasons (monetary value, importance in the history of printing, binding, association interest—e.g., presidential inaugural Bibles—or fragility), they have one point in common: their long-term scholarly interest. Particular strengths in this general rare-book collection are Cervantes, ballooning, early city directories, and English and American literature.

The remaining two thirds of the division's holdings have been organized into separately maintained collections, of which the following will serve as examples:

Heavy bronze doors guard the entrance to the area on the second floor of the main building occupied by the Rare Book Division. The door panels carry the names or devices of eminent printers and book designers.

personal libraries (Thomas Jefferson, Woodrow Wilson, Theodore Roosevelt, Susan B. Anthony, Oliver Wendell Holmes, and Harry Houdini); comprehensive author collections (Walt Whitman, Henry James, Sigmund Freud, Rudyard Kipling, Benjamin Franklin, and Hans Christian Andersen); history of papermaking (Harrison Elliott Collection); type design (the personal library of Frederic W. Goudy); subject collections (magic, gastronomy, cryptography); early Russian and Bulgarian imprints; the illustrated book (the internationally known collection formed by the late Lessing J. Rosenwald); collections with unusual provenance (Russian Imperial and Third Reich collections); and generic collections (miniature books, Bibles, American children's books,

This manuscript, the work of a French scribe, may date from the year 1470, which makes it one of the oldest of the rare books in the Library of Congress. It is open to an illustration of the slaying of the giant Goliath by David.

broadsides, theater playbills, pre-1871 copyright records, documents of the first fourteen Congresses, dime novels, Hawaiian imprints, and Confederate States imprints).

The division's holdings of more than 5,600 incunabula (books printed before 1501) constitute the largest such assemblage in the Western Hemisphere. Americana is another overriding strength, dating from the Columbus Letter of 1493 to the present and including more than 16,000 imprints from the period 1640 to 1800, Western Americana, and thousands of nineteenth-century pamphlets.

Some of the treasures of the Rare Book and Special Collections Division were purchased by the Library of Congress. In 1929, for example, the Library acquired 3,000 fifteenth-century books, including the Gutenberg Bible on display, for the remarkably low sum of $1.5 million. Other books have come to the division as gifts. Rosenwald has given the Library of Congress a number of outstanding examples of early printing, as well as the famous Giant Bible of Mainz and a beautiful collection of finely illustrated books dating from the fifteenth century to the twentieth. Another valuable donation is the Alfred Whital Stern Collection of Lincolniana, which contains not only manuscripts and printed material but also such Lincoln memorabilia as a razor once used to shave the Civil War President.

Since 1929, when the Library acquired it, the Gutenberg Bible has been displayed in the Great Hall of the main building.

The Gutenberg Bible being viewed by former Austrian Chancellor Julius Raab was printed on vellum at Mainz, Germany, between 1450 and 1456. Raab toured the Library five centuries later, in 1954.

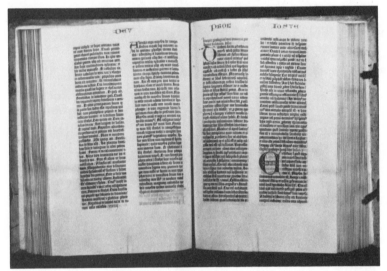

Close-up of the Gutenberg Bible. Note the two devices on the right edge to hold the book closed.

A portion of the stack area housing the Rare Book Division's incunabula (books printed before the year 1501).

A manuscript book containing some of the writings of St. Thomas Aquinas still bears the chain that fastened it to a reading stand in a German monastery.

Journals of the Congress, in thirteen volumes, formerly the property of George Washington, is one of many important historical works in the Library. The first president's bookplate can be seen at the left.

Il Federalista, Italian edition of an English book, was presented to Librarian Mumford *(left)* by Italian President Giovanni Gronchi in 1956. In exchange, Mumford gave him the English translation of *The Florentine Fior di Virtu of 1491.* The rare Florentine edition was published for the Library by Lessing J. Rosenwald of Jenkintown, Pennsylvania.

These readers are using the Rare Book Division's collection of American newspapers of the 1780s.

The division's Alfred Whital Stern Collection of Lincolniana contains this letter written in 1863 by President Lincoln to his newly appointed Commander of the Army of the Potomac, General Joseph Hooker.

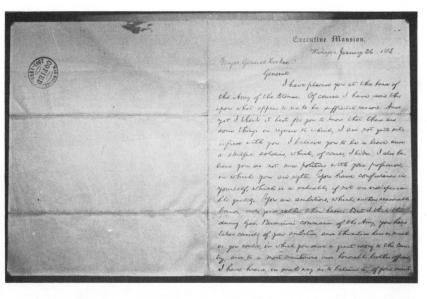

Facsimile editions of two rare books printed in Paris before 1500—*The Dance of Death* and *Le Chevalier Délibéré*—were presented to King Mohamed V of Morocco in 1957. He also received a copy of *Image of America,* a collection of early American photographs, from Librarian L. Quincy Mumford. Looking on *(right)* is Abderrahman Naggai, chief of the Royal Cabinet.

In late 1944, the thirteen-foot-long Articles of Confederation was removed from the bombproof secret crypt where it had been stored with other documents for safety during World War II. Librarian Archibald MacLeish *(center)* examines it with members of his staff. *Associated Press Photo*

Books in this exhibit case were once in Thomas Jefferson's library at Monticello.

This cover features a Christian cross and the letters *IHS*.

Miniature books are stored in a series of drawers.

These two copies of Omar Khayyám's *Rose Garden*, printed in Worcester, Massachusetts, in 1932, are among the smallest volumes in the Rare Book Division.

"Ten-cent novels" were popular sellers in the nineteenth century. *The Poisoned Letter,* however, sold at the inflated price of twenty-five cents in 1867.

Miniature and small books, including these being viewed by comedian Danny Kaye, are often displayed by the Rare Book and Special Collections Division. The division also collects children's books and dime novels.

In 1889, while visiting in Pennsylvania, Rudyard Kipling composed verses about six different fruits and painted them on white dessert plates. The six plates, later mounted in a binding said to have cost $2,500, are now in the Carpenter Kipling Collection of the Rare Book Division.

Scholars working with the Library's collection of rare printed materials use this special reading room on the second floor of the main building.

All patrons of the Rare Book Room must fill out a special registration form and agree to comply with the rules.

A letter from magician Harry Houdini describing one of his 1926 experiments is presented by James M. Day, of the Department of the Interior, to Acting Librarian John G. Lorenz. The letter was accepted in 1975 for the Rare Book and Special Collections Division, which houses many Houdini items.

Artist-naturalist John James Audubon's *Birds of America*, open at an engraving of a raven, is one of the treasures of the Library of Congress.

Among the curios in the Stern Collection of Lincolniana is a life mask of Lincoln's political rival, Stephen A. Douglas.

Autographed books by W. Somerset Maugham *(seated)* are included in the more than half-million volumes in the division.

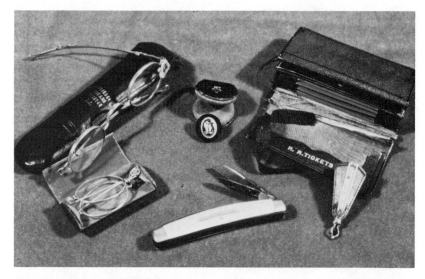

President Lincoln had these items in his pockets the night he was shot at Ford's Theater. They are part of the Rare Book and Special Collections Division.

Papers of most of the presidents from George Washington through Calvin Coolidge are available on microfilm.

From the Wilson papers, here is an early draft of his Fourteen Points for a post–World War I settlement.

HANDWRITTEN RECORDS OF THE NATION'S PAST

Manuscripts in the Library of Congress collections take a number of forms. There are letters, journals and diaries, notebooks, drafts of speeches and articles, orderly books, logs, memoranda—written documents of every kind that have to do with individuals, organizations, or events important to the history of the United States.

Most of the collections in the Manuscript Division have been acquired since 1897, and many of them came to the Library as gifts from generous benefactors. The personal papers of twenty-three Presidents from Washington through Coolidge are now in the Manuscript Division on 3,000 reels of microfilm. Also available are the papers of Alexander Hamilton, Benjamin Franklin, John Paul Jones, the Wright brothers, Samuel Morse, Susan B. Anthony, and Clare Boothe Luce—to mention just a few of the individuals represented. Altogether, the 32 million or so pieces on file in the division represent an unequaled source of firsthand information for students of American history.

The Manuscript Division's Presidential Papers Program conducts the arranging, indexing, and microfilming of the papers of twenty-three presidents. This staff member is working on the papers of President Theodore Roosevelt.

Executive Mansion,

Washington,   , 186

Four score and seven years ago our fathers brought forth, upon this continent, a new nation, conceived in liberty, and dedicated to the proposition that "all men are created equal"

Now we are engaged in a great civil war, testing whether that nation, or any nation so conceived and so dedicated, can long endure. We are met on a great battle field of that war. We have come to dedicate a portion of it, as a final re...

Here is a portion of the Gettysburg Address in President Lincoln's own hand.

Former President Harry S Truman reads Lincoln's Farewell Address to Springfield in the stacks of the Manuscript Division. The speech was written in pencil on the train as Lincoln began his journey to Washington for his first inauguration in 1861. On this occasion in 1957, Truman visited the Library prior to testifying on its behalf before a congressional committee. David C. Mearns of the Library staff holds the book.

This drawing, made by President Ulysses S. Grant when he was a West Point cadet, is in the collection of his papers.

Before a president's papers can be microfilmed, they must be sorted and arranged by the division staff.

The reading room of the Manuscript Division, located in the Adams Building, has ample facilities for many researchers of handwritten documents.

This pre-1939 photograph of Sigmund Freud is from the collection of his papers maintained by the Library. A portion of one of his letters is also shown here.

As far as I can remember these are the first sketches of my Telephone — or instrument for the transmission of vocal utterances by telegraph.

A. Graham

Alexander Graham Bell wrote that, as far as he could remember, this is the first drawing made of his telephone.

Palm leaves form the basis of several manuscripts from Thailand, including the one being held and the one shown in close-up.

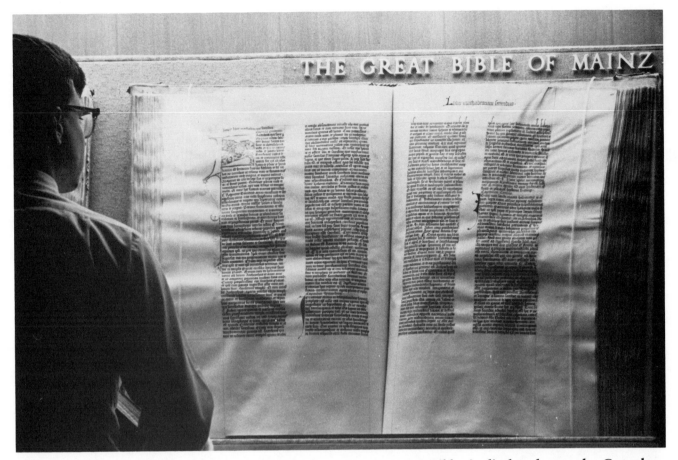

The Great Bible of Mainz, a 500-year-old illuminated manuscript Bible, is displayed near the Gutenberg Bible.

This handwritten document proclaiming Maine's statehood in 1820 was part of a special display honoring the state's sesquicentennial. Then Governor and Mrs. Kenneth M. Curtis are shown reading it in 1971. Ten years before, Governor Curtis had worked for the Congressional Research Service.

In 1951, then Princess Elizabeth of England viewed the Declaration of Independence at the Library. It had been in the custody of the Manuscript Division from 1897 to 1952 when the Declaration and the U.S. Constitution were transferred to the nearby National Archives.

The rebus or hieroglyphic letter was popular in France and England during the seventeenth and eighteenth centuries. Matthew Darly published this rebus on May 11, 1778, in London, indicating the Colonists' strong determination for independence. The title reads, "America to her mistaken mother."

First editions of compositions by Ludwig van Beethoven, Joseph Haydn, and Wolfgang Amadeus Mozart were presented to the Music Division in 1952 by then mayor of Vienna, Franz Jonas *(right).* Also admiring the works are *(left to right)* Dr. Ernest Lachs, city manager of Vienna; Luther H. Evans, Librarian of Congress; and Harold Spivacke, chief of the Music Division.

MUSIC FOR AMERICA

The history of the Music Division goes back to the reorganization of 1897, when it emerged as a separate department charged with caring for a collection of 250,000 musical scores and songs and the 15,000 additional pieces that come to the Library annually as copyright deposits. Over the years the Music Division has expanded its holdings and activities. Today its collections include more than 3.6 million musical scores, 512,000 books and pamphlets about music, and 796,000 musical recordings in the form of disks, tapes, and wires. The division has also become the active sponsor of both the creation and the performance of good music. Some thirty to forty concerts each year at the Library are made possible by gifts and endowments that the Music Division has received from the Elizabeth Sprague Coolidge, Gertrude Clark Whittall, Serge Koussevitzky, Norman P. Scala, and the McKim funds.

In 1979 more than 22,000 musicians, students of music, and representatives of government agencies and the music industry sought assistance from the staff of the Music Division on subjects ranging from folk music to grand opera. Thousands more attended concerts sponsored by the Library of Congress. One of the special concerts in 1978 was the premiere of "The Library of Congress March" by J. William Middendorf II, performed by the U.S. Navy Ceremonial Band. (Middendorf had served as Secretary of the Navy.)

When not in use, the Library's Stradivari violins, with a viola and a cello also made by the great Italian craftsman, are stored in a specially ventilated case in the Whittall Pavilion, which adjoins the Library's Coolidge Auditorium.

Close-up view of a Stradivari violin displayed at the Library.

International in scope and spanning many centuries, the collections are sufficiently rich and voluminous to provide a basis for the most penetrating research. Manuscript sources include autographed scores and letters by composers and musicians from the time of Bach to the present day. Numerous microfilm reproductions and facsimiles of rare and unique resources are available. The collection of periodicals is probably unmatched in the world.

Every type of printed music is represented in the collections, from the classics to rock-and-roll. Books are available on all aspects of musical documentation, covering such diverse fields as history, biography, esthetics, philosophy, psychology, and organology, to mention only a few. Pedagogical literature on file includes methods and studies for every instrument and voice, as well as manuals for the entire field of music education, and textbooks on harmony, counterpoint, form and analysis, orchestration, and conducting.

Copyright deposits represent the largest share of the Music Division's annual acquisitions. Additional materials are obtained through purchase, gift, exchange, and transfer. The division maintains a particularly fine collection of all types of American music, both serious and popular, from all periods of U.S. history.

Holographic scores in the collection include Bach's Cantata No. 9, which he composed in 1731.

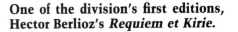

Among the Library's 3.6 million musical scores is the score for Walt Disney Productions' immortal *Bambi*.

One of the division's first editions, Hector Berlioz's *Requiem et Kirie*.

A student at work in the Music Reading Room. Behind her is a writing desk designed and used by composer Gershwin.

George Gershwin's autograph is one of the many prized items in the music collection.

The Music Reading Room also displays a desk and chair that belonged to the composer Sergei Rachmaninoff.

Benjamin Britten's manuscript copy of his Quartet No. 1 in D Major is displayed with a violin made by Kreisler Guarnerius on the desk once owned by Rachmaninoff.

Some of the treasures of the Music Division are shown off by Barbara Henry for Prince and Princess Hitachi of Japan in 1978.

A page from the prized *Ephrata Codex*, a book of music in manuscript form.

Musical instruments from Thailand were given to the division by King Bhumibol Adulyadej *(left)*. An accomplished musician, the King has been known to sit in with Western bands.

This reader is examining some of the Music Division's rare editions. Books in the collections range from volumes just published to fifteenth-century works.

Using Stradivari instruments given to the Library by Mrs. Gertrude Clarke Whittall, the Juilliard Quartet performs in the Coolidge Auditorium. A regular concert series has been held in the Library since 1925, when the auditorium, the gift of Mrs. Elizabeth Sprague Coolidge, was added to the main building.

Behind the scenes in the Music Division. Locked cases for the division's rare books are on the left.

Original manuscripts of chamber music commissioned by the Elizabeth Sprague Coolidge Foundation are displayed in the foyer of the Coolidge Auditorium.

Music mementos presented to the Library by Mrs. Whittall are displayed in the Whittall Pavilion, added to the main building in 1937 as another gift.

Mrs. Whittall also furnished the Poetry Room on the third floor of the main building. The room is used for small poetry readings sponsored by the Library.

Several funds sponsor programs and recitals in the Coolidge Auditorium.

William Meredith, Poetry Consultant for the Library, recites some of his works in the Coolidge Auditorium. Such programs normally are open to the public.

An assistant in the Poetry Room examines a manuscript poem by Robert Frost.

A member of the Japanese Section examines a sample of the world's oldest known printing, a Buddhist charm, or *dharani*, printed in Japan between A.D. 764 and A.D. 770. The pagoda *(left)*, which also dates to the same period, was made especially to hold a *dharani*.

THE ASIAN AND AFRICAN AND MIDDLE EASTERN DIVISIONS

Since World War II, Asia and the Arab world have been much in the news, and the result for the Library of Congress has been a steady increase in requests for information. Population and political divisions in North Vietnam, the flora of Thailand, the state of roads and transportation in Indonesia, the whereabouts of three Samaritan Pentateuch manuscripts, a list of the unpublished Arabic works of the tenth-century scholar Yefet ben 'Ali—these are samples of the reference requests received, and answered. For Congress the divisions have translated letters, newspaper articles, and documents into and from such languages as Hebrew, Yiddish, Vietnamese, Hindi, and Urdu.

The divisions administer the Library's extensive collections of Chinese, Korean, Japanese, Hebraic, Near Eastern, and South Asian materials and are staffed by specialists in these literatures. The Chinese collections, which are the largest outside China, began in 1869 with a gift of 933 volumes from the Emperor of China. The collections now contain 441,000 volumes and include a Buddhist sutra printed in A.D. 975 as well as books, newspapers, and periodicals from China. In the 65,000-volume Korean collection the emphasis is on recent publications from both North and South Korea.

In addition to a large number of works dealing with the literature, history, and institutions of Japan, the Japanese collections of the Library of Congress include such items as microfilm reproductions of the archives of the Japanese Ministry of Foreign Affairs from 1868 to 1945, the publications of the South Manchuria Railway Company, and material issued by the Thought Control Police of the prewar Home Ministry. Of the more than 606,000 volumes in the Japanese collections, the largest outside the Orient, those dealing with science and technology are most often requested in applications for loan or photoduplication.

The Hebraic collections of the Library of Congress include works of Hebrew, Yiddish, Ladino, Syriac, Aramaic, Judeo-Arabic, Judeo-Persian, Amharic, and Geez—some 114,000 books and pamphlets in all. The Library of Congress is particularly noted for its collections of

The Buddhist charms were produced in strip format, shown here being examined.

Shown above are two volumes of a twenty-four-volume seventeenth-century Japanese picture book. The set contains 111 full-page illustrations and was written in black ink with a brush.

bibliographic reference works pertaining to Israel and Ethiopia, official publications of those countries, and modern Hebrew and Yiddish literary works. Its materials dealing with Bible study and Hebraic, Yiddish, and Ethiopian cultures are also considered outstanding.

During 1978, for instance, the African and Middle Eastern Division prepared five bibliographies with a total of 3,269 entries. They included *Uganda: Subject Guide to Official Publications* and *Islam in Sub-Saharan Africa: A Partially Annotated Guide*. During that same year, nearly 11,300 volumes of division material were used in the Library and 675 others were loaned to other libraries. More than 20,000 people made use of the division's reference service.

The Library's collections of Africana, initially supported by a generous grant from the Carnegie Corporation, are among the best in the world. They encompass every major field of study except technical agriculture and clinical medicine (which are under the jurisdiction of the National Agricultural Library and the National Library of Medicine, respectively). Most of the materials, including especially strong holdings in economics, history, linguistics, and literature, are dispersed in the Library's general book and periodical collections. How-

Texts dealing with archeology and Hebraism were of special interest to Japanese Prince Mikasa when he toured the Library in 1965. Notice the Japanese characters on the books in the background. More than 606,000 such volumes are included in the collection of the Asian Division, including several written by Prince Mikasa.

ever, an additional wealth of Africana may be found in special collections of legal material, manuscripts, maps, microfilm, music, newspapers, prints, photographs, and films in various custodial divisions of the Library. The African and Middle Eastern Division's primary roles are to continue to develop these collections, assist researchers in locating material, and compile bibliographic guides which will bring its holdings to the attention of librarians and scholars.

Congressional offices, the State and Commerce departments, the Bureau of the Census, and the "Voice of America" make frequent use of the division's volumes in the languages of the Near and Middle East, which include works in Azerbaijani, Kazakh, Georgian, and Uzbek, as well as in the more common Arabic, Turkish, and Persian.

Like the Near East collections, which contain a good representation of classical Turkish and Arabic works, the South Asian collections are a mixture of the old and the new. Several hundred Sanskrit books and forty volumes that were among the first to be printed in Bengal in the eighteenth century share shelf space with recent publications acquired through postwar purchasing programs. Materials dealing with political science, economics, technology, and foreign relations are most in demand.

Woodblock prints such as these two by Utamaro (1753–1806) are part of the Japanese collection.

The Library of Congress receives Japanese daily newspapers in monthly book form. Because they are printed photographically in reduced size, a magnifying glass makes reading easier.

A staff member of the Chinese Section reads an encyclopedia prepared during the time of Emperor Yung-lo of the Ming Dynasty (1368–1644).

Two representatives of the Republic of China admire an ancient Chinese scroll with Library staff members. The scroll, printed in A.D. 975, is the earliest specimen of Chinese printing in the Library.

One of the thousands of books in the Korean collection is held by then South Korean Ambassador to the United States, You Chan Yang. He was at the Library in 1953 to view a collection of materials acquired by Mrs. Evelyn McClure in his country. Looking on are Pyo Wook Han, counselor of the Korean Embassy, and Librarian Luther H. Evans. The extra hands in the display case are reflections.

A staff member displays some of the more than 36,000 volumes in the vernacular languages of South and Southeast Asia.

In June 1869 "His Majesty the Emperor of China" presented a volume on "Chinese Herbal" medicine to the government of the United States of America.

Here is a sampling of the Asian Division's many books and periodicals from remote Nepal. Virtually every area of the world is represented in the Library's collections. King Mahendra looks over Queen Ratna's shoulder as she reads a Nepali newspaper.

The Dalai Lama *(left)* examines Tibetan texts during his 1979 visit to the Library.

Librarian Archibald MacLeish hosted Saudi Princes Amir Faisal and Amir Khalid. They review an ancient scroll containing the genealogy of the Prophet Mohammed, through his favorite daughter, Fatima, and continuing through her husband Ali for twenty-six generations to 1798. It is substantiated by fourteen seals, starting with Mohammed's.

Samples of Arabic calligraphy are included in the collections of the Near East Section.

Gilt inscription above the statue of Commerce in the Main Reading Room. One of eight.

One of the more than 114,000 items in the Hebraic collections of the African-Middle Eastern Division.

Another ancient scroll is Isaac ben Abba Mari's *Safer ha-Itur,* published in 1608 in Venice.

Publications from Africa and others produced by the Library are housed in its Africana collections.

The largest collection of Slavic books in the Western world is held by the European Division.

THE EUROPEAN DIVISION

The European Division, now the home of the largest collection of books in the Slavic languages in the Western world, had only 569 Russian books in 1901, and few of them were standard works. In 1907, however, the Library acquired 80,000 volumes relating to Russia and Siberia from Gennadius Vasilievich Yudin, a wealthy Siberian book collector. The books, all but 12,000 of them in the Russian language, became the nucleus of the present outstanding collection in all the Slavic languages.

The Bicentennial of the American Revolution figured prominently in the department's services to Congress, government agencies, and researchers and in the Library's publications program. Nearly every division received many inquiries relating to the American Revolution, including many from abroad. To cite only a few examples, the European Division assisted in research on East Europeans who participated in the Revolution, the reaction among their compatriots at home, and the subsequent development of American studies in these lands. Inquiries were received concerning Colonel Michael de Kovats (a Hungarian who distinguished

The title page of one of the books in the Slavic Room—*The Russian Icon,* a collection of articles published in St. Petersburg in 1914.

Foreign-language newspapers are readily available in the reading room.

Journals, magazines, and newspapers in a number of languages pour into the European Division.

The attitude of American leaders toward Poland in 1776 and today is documented in collections of the European Division.

Part of a page from a four-volume history of the Russian cavalry guard, once in the private library of Gennadius Vasilievich Yudin.

himself in the battle of Charleston), the attitudes of America's founding fathers toward Poland, Jefferson's observations on German wines, and Serbs who fought with the patriot army.

In recent years the reference services of the European Division were used by about 30,000 people annually, with approximately half of their inquiries made by telephone. During the latter half of the 1970s, circulation of European Division items within the Library increased from 22,600 to 60,000 annually.

A letter from Benjamin Franklin to the Court of Versailles in 1784 and an original copy of the first treaty between Austria and the United States in 1829 were presented to the Library in 1952. Librarian Luther H. Evans accepts the documents from Austrian Chancellor Leopold Figl. The "Voice of America" broadcasted the ceremony to Austria.

THE HISPANIC DIVISION

Several decades of interest on the part of the Library of Congress in the Hispanic and Portuguese cultures, combined with the support and encouragement of Archer M. Huntington, noted Hispanist and past president of the Hispanic Society of America, led to the formation, in 1939, of what is now the Hispanic Division. Originally known as the Hispanic Foundation in the Library of Congress, the division was established as a center for the pursuit of studies in the cultures of Latin America, the Iberian peninsula, and those areas where the influence of the Iberian peninsula has been significant, particularly the Philippines and the southwestern part of the United States. The division serves Congress, federal agencies, the scholarly community, and the general public.

The Library's Hispanic and Portuguese collections are among the best in the world and represent resources that have been increasing for more than a century and a half. All major subject areas are represented; the collections are especially strong in history, literature, and the social sciences. Of the more than 18 million volumes in the general book collections of the Library, an estimated 1 million volumes are concerned with Hispanic and Portuguese culture. The collections are not housed in the division, but are in the general collections of the Library. Besides the general book collections, other major collections relating to Latin America include manuscripts, government publications, newspapers, periodicals, legal materials, maps, prints and photographs, and music—also housed separately in various divisions of the Library. The Hispanic Division's primary role is to develop these collections and to explain and interpret them through published guides and bibliographies for the benefit of students, scholars, and libraries—much as the other area studies divisions do.

The Hispanic Reading Room has limited study space with priority given to those engaged in Hispanic and Portuguese studies.

Candido Portnari painted four murals depicting the history of the Latin American people, as shown here in the Jefferson Building. For a perspective of the size of these two murals, note the chair in the corner.

A student of Spanish researches in the Hispanic Reading Room, one of seventeen reading rooms in the Library.

The marble plaque beneath the ornate shield commemorates the founding in 1939 of the Hispanic Foundation in the Library of Congress, now the Hispanic Division.

History, literature, and the social sciences are especially strong areas of the Hispanic Division.

Spanish and Portuguese literature may be read and heard, as shown here, through the resources of the Hispanic Division. Its Archive of Hispanic Literature on Tape is located in the Jefferson Building.

GEOGRAPHY AND MAP DIVISION

United States maps predominate in the Library map collections. But topographic, geologic, climatic, soil, vegetation, mineral resource, population, transportation, and other special subject maps are available for most countries of the world.

Established as the Hall of Maps and Charts when the main building of the Library of Congress was opened in 1897, the Geography and Map Division is one of seventeen divisions of the Library's Research Services department. As the collections grew it became necessary to move the division to larger quarters, first to the 1939 Annex and, in October 1969, to a building on South Pickett Street in Alexandria, Virginia, about twelve miles from the Library of Congress complex. Then in early 1980, the Geography and Map Division returned to Capitol Hill and the new James Madison Memorial Building. Its facilities include a well-equipped reading room. The relocation of more than 3.5 million sheets and volumes of maps took more than a month.

Among the earliest original manuscript maps in the collection are three portolano (navigational) atlases and seventeen portolano charts from the fourteenth through seventeenth centuries drawn on vellum by Italian, Portuguese, and Spanish cartographers. The excellent condition of the atlases dates from the earliest printed editions of Ptolemy's *Geography* (1482) and includes representative volumes of all significant publishers of atlases of the last five centuries. The atlases cover individual continents, countries, states, counties, and cities, as well as the world. They range in scope from comprehensive to topical.

Hand-colored woodblocks are featured in this 1482 edition of Claudius Ptolemy's atlas. Africa is the area in the bottom left.

Of particular interest to genealogists and local historians is a large collection of U.S. county and state atlases published in the last half of the nineteenth century. Atlases published during the past four or five decades and covering national, regional, state, and provincial resources form another noteworthy reference group. The collection of single maps embraces more than 1.5 million general and special subject maps of the world and its various political entities, divisions, and subdivisions.

Plans of a fortified European town along the Vechte River are in the Geography and Map Division.

Maps of the heavens as drawn by early astronomers also included elaborate celestial figures.

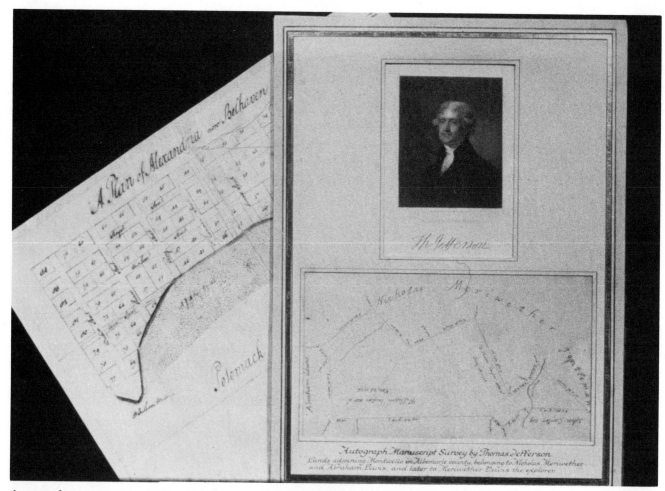

Apprentice surveyor George Washington laid out the lots on John Alexander's farm along the Potomac River and thus drew the foundation for Alexandria, Virginia. On top of that map is another survey with a portrait of Thomas Jefferson.

About 3.5 million maps, 38,000 atlases, and 8,000 reference books are available to users of the Map Reading Room.

In 1803 a London printer produced a set of thirty-two cards containing a geographical description of the world. Each card was embellished with costumed people representing a given area.

Maps from around the globe are collected by the Geography and Map Division. Shown here is a decorative map of Ethiopia being discussed by then Emperor Haile Selassie and Acting Librarian of Congress Verner E. Clapp.

Two Science and Technology Division staff members examine a bibliography, one of the division's many contributions to the literature of science.

Materials in the Science and Technology Division range from technical reports to botanical drawings. The aerospace collections are world famous.

SERVICE TO THE NATION'S SCIENTISTS AND SCHOLARS

The Library of Congress responded to the many scientific and technological developments that have taken place since World War II by greatly expanding its holdings and services in these fields. In addition to over 3 million books and 20,000 journals, it makes available to scientists and researchers all the unclassified reports of the Atomic Energy Commission, the Department of Defense, and the National Aeronautics and Space Administration, dealing with research performed under government contract, and thousands of other valuable domestic and foreign technical reports. The Library's collections of aerospace literature in manuscript and printed form are the largest in the world and still growing.

The staff of the Science and Technology Division prepares numerous studies for Congress and other government agencies on such subjects as weather modification, strontium 90 contamination, and Soviet fisheries research, but perhaps the most important service provided by the division is its contract bibliography program. Any agency or organization can, for a fee, request a bibliography on a scientific or technical subject. The division, using the book, periodical, and report resources of the Library of Congress, will prepare a comprehensive survey of the literature on that subject.

Another important service that the Library of Congress provides for the nation's scientists and scholars is its National Referral Center. The center handles referrals in virtually all subject areas, including the arts and humanities. It maintains a computerized file of 13,000 organizations for resources mainly in the United States. An information resource is broadly defined to include any organization, institution, group, or individual with specialized information in a particular field and a willingness to share it with others. This includes not only traditional sources of information, such as techni-

Display panels are prepared for shipment for the Science and Technology Division.

cal libraries, information and documentation centers, and abstracting and indexing services, but also such sources as professional societies, university research bureaus and institutes, government agencies, industrial laboratories, museums, testing stations, hobby groups, and grass-roots citizens' organizations. The criteria for registering are not size but ability and willingness to provide information on a reasonable basis.

Buffalo Bill's Wild West Show lives again on posters stored at the Library.

Niagara Falls is the subject of an ambrotype *(positive on glass)* made around 1854 and still preserved in its original case.

GRAPHIC AMERICANA AND OTHER SIMILAR AREAS

The prints and photographs collections of the Library of Congress provide a visual record of people, places, and events in America and throughout the world. The Prints and Photographs Division maintains custody of these extensive holdings, which number more than 10 million prints, photographs, negatives, posters, and other pictorial materials. Many of the items are in the public domain and therefore are available for various uses. The general collection provides a pictorial record of American and world political, social, and cultural history from 1860 to the present.

The division includes fine and historical prints, master photographs, architectural collections, posters, reference and loan services, as well as a superb mail-order photocopying service.

The historical print collection contains 40,000 lithographs, engravings, woodcuts, and other original prints which illustrate eighteenth- and nineteenth-century life in America and Europe. The period from the fifteenth century to the present is represented by the fine-print collection, which consists of 110,000 items. They represent the works of artists in major countries throughout the world.

Some pictorial material, such as this collection of rare sixteenth-century chiaroscuro woodcuts, is in album form.

Early daguerreotypes to contemporary portfolios make up the 3,500 original images in the master photographers collection. The architectural collections of more than 100,000 items form the most comprehensive architectural archive in the United States. The holdings include the photographic records of the Historic American Engineering Record, the Pictorial Archives of Early American Architecture, the Carnegie Survey of the Architecture of the South, and various supplemental collections. In addition, there is a fine collection of original architectural drawings.

Sixty thousand American and foreign posters ranging from the 1850s to the present comprise the poster collection. Covering a wide variety of subjects, the collection includes war, propaganda, political, art exhibition, travel, and theatrical posters, and motion picture and circus advertisements, as well as Art Nouveau and magazine posters. There are also Austrian and German Expressionist posters, original silk-screen display posters produced by the Work Projects Administration between 1936 and 1941, and posters by contemporary artists.

Researchers may consult the collections in the Prints and Photographs Reading Room. There are also reference specialists available for assistance. Photocopies of materials in the division that are not under copyright or other restrictions may be ordered through the photocopying service. Price lists are available from the Library of Congress, Photoduplication Service, Washington, D.C. 20540.

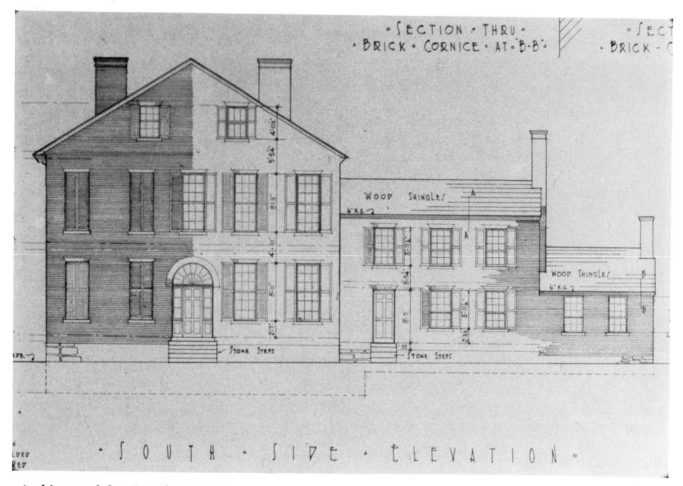

Architectural drawing of an early American mansion.

Pictorial items requested by readers are delivered to their study tables in the Prints and Photographs Reading Room.

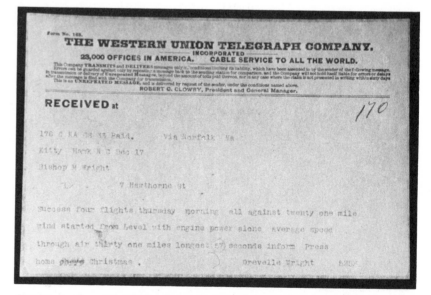

On December 17, 1903, the aviation pioneers sent this telegram to their father, Bishop M. Wright, at 7 Hawthorne Street, Dayton, Ohio. It reads: "Success four flights thursday morning all against twenty one mile wind started from Level with engine power alone average speed through air thirty one miles longest 57 seconds inform Press home Christmas." The telegram is stored in the Manuscripts Division.

Shown is a selection of data sheets and file photographs from the Historic American Building Survey.

This intaglio print by Stanley William Hayter is an example of the Library's contemporary art in the Pennell Collection.

Two staff members examine the original copper plate of an etching by the American artist Joseph Pennell. Pennell, who died in 1926, left $314,000 to the Library for the purchase of prints "of the greatest excellence only."

This negative of General Custer is one of 10,000 in the Brady-Handy Collection, taken by Matthew Brady and his nephew, Levin C. Handy, in the decades after the Civil War.

Photographs of Civil War Union generals in the Brady Collection line the file cabinets in the area where negatives of famous pictures are stored.

History of the Civil War in action photographs.

Collection of the Farm Security Administration.   **A mood study of actress Greta Garbo.**

Early advertisements such as this can be studied in the commercial and graphic arts collections of the Prints and Photographs Division.

More than 10 million pictorial items are maintained by the Prints and Photographs Division. Copies of those in the public domain are available for sale. Examples from the collection also are shown on these pages.

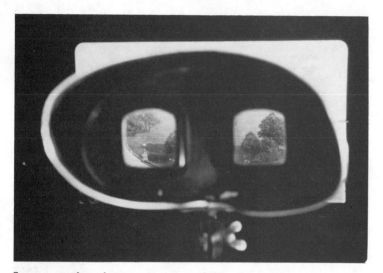

Stereoscopic viewers are available for researchers who study history as presented on stereograph cards.

Orville and Wilbur Wright brought their own camera to Kitty Hawk, North Carolina, to record the first powered, controlled, and sustained flight. Their original negative is maintained by the Prints and Photographs Division.

The Library also has this item of aviation history—a dollar bill carried by Charles A. Lindbergh on his 1927 flight across the Atlantic Ocean. He signed it in two places and inscripted it to Harold M. Bixby.

Souvenir pictures from the 1939 World's Fair in New York City.

Two staff members display one of the many posters in the division's collection.

Mrs. William Boyd presents to Librarian Daniel J. Boorstin a poster that reproduces a portrait of her late husband, who was known to millions of television and movie viewers as "Hopalong Cassidy." The poster, presented in 1977, was autographed by a number of Western stars including John Wayne, Ronald Reagan, Randolph Scott, Jack Elam, Andy Devine, and Dale Robertson.

AN AUDIO-VISUAL DIVISION

These disks represent an early form of the motion picture. As they are rotated, the designs appear to move.

A new division was formed in 1978 by combining the Recorded Sound Section of the Music Division and the Motion Picture Section of the Prints and Photographs Division. They became the Motion Picture, Broadcasting, and Recorded Sound Division. Its work emphasizes not only films, but also acquisitions, preservations, and reference activities in the radio and television broadcasting field, thus fulfilling a mandate of the new Copyright Act. During its first year as a new organization, the division assisted researchers by circulating nearly 26,000 items within the Library and loaned nearly 6,000 to other libraries. It also handled 11,439 direct reference requests—more than half by telephone. In its second year, the direct references were more than 22,000 requests.

The Library of Congress motion picture collections began, literally, with a sneeze. In 1894, the moving picture *Edison Kinetoscopic Record of a Sneeze*, better known as *Fred Ott's Sneeze*, was deposited for copyright. Because there was no provision in the copyright laws for the registration of moving pictures, *Fred Ott's Sneeze* and other early films were treated as pictorial material and deposited in the form of photographs printed on rolls of paper. In 1912, the laws were amended to permit the registration of motion pictures as a distinct form. During the next thirty years, however, because of the difficulty of handling the highly flammable nitrate film used at the time, the Library retained only descriptive materials relating to motion pictures. This practice changed in 1942, when, recognizing the importance of motion pictures and the need to preserve them as a historical record, the Library began to retain films.

The collections today contain 80,000 titles, or more than 281,000 reels. More than 1,200 titles, including television films and video tapes, are added each year through copyright deposit, purchase, gift, or exchange. The collections also include more than 300,000 stills.

The preservation of its motion picture collections is a prime concern of the Library. Film—whether in the form of paper prints, nitrate, or acetate—is one of the most fragile of all art mediums. In 1948, the Academy of Motion Picture Arts and Sciences sponsored a project to develop a practical method of converting paper prints—

A view of the stacks area in the Adams Building where the motion-picture collection is maintained. Other government agencies and private corporations copy 50,000 feet of film annually when the film is in the public domain or when copyright owners grant permission.

which are difficult to examine and impossible to project—to acetate (safety) film. After a technique was perfected, the Academy paid for the conversion of 1,600 titles in the Library's collections, and in 1958, the Congress appropriated funds to continue the project to its conclusion in 1964.

In the early 1960s, the Library began efforts to restore motion pictures that were made on highly combustible nitrate film—footage that must be stored in fireproof vaults outside the District of Columbia, some as far away as Wright-Patterson Air Force Base, Ohio. Its efforts were enhanced in 1970, when, with assistance from the American Film Institute, the Library installed a sophisticated motion picture preservation laboratory in its main building. In the laboratory, old nitrate film is cleaned by an ultrasonic process, repaired, and transferred frame by frame to acetate stock. The film that is being converted is stored in a small fireproof vault in the laboratory. The facility is capable of converting more than 4 million feet of film each year. A design contract was let in 1979 to construct a new nitrate film conversion laboratory at Wright-Patterson Air Force Base.

In his capacity as a member of the National Council for the Arts, actor Gregory Peck examines motion-picture footage stored at the Library. Early films were saved in the form of individual photographs printed in series on rolls of paper.

The Recorded Sound Section is responsible for custody and service of all sound recordings in the Library, regardless of subject, with the exception of "talking books," for which the National Library Service for the Blind and Physically Handicapped is responsible. Facilities for listening to sound recordings are made available on request to persons doing serious research.

Directors as well as actors visit the Motion Picture Section, now part of Motion Picture, Broadcasting, and Recorded Sound Division. Rouben Mamoulian sought out Thomas Edison's thirty-second 1894 film *The Sneeze* in the movie archives during his 1968 tour. Mamoulian directed such movies as *Silk Stockings* and *Blood and Sand* and such stage plays as *Porgy* and *Oklahoma!*

Dolores Del Rio enjoys watching scenes from the movie *The Fugitive,* in which she starred. Shown with her during a 1967 visit to the Motion Picture Section are *(left to right)* John B. Kuiper, section head; Guillermo Davila, a cousin of Miss Del Rio; and Lewis A. Riley, her husband. The posters in the background are part of the 60,000 placards in the Library collection.

More than 281,000 reels of film are included in the division's collection. Here a sound print is examined on a viewing machine.

A disk from the old "Shadow" radio program is reviewed by a researcher in the Recorded Sound Section.

The Library recording collections include some items that date back to the days of the Edison cylinder *(left)*. This cylinder phonograph *(above)* is part of the recording laboratory's equipment.

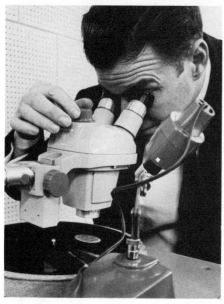

The recording laboratory studio in action.

The recording laboratory maintains a high standard for its products. Here an engineer checks the grooves of a newly cut disk.

Cutting lathes and turntables of the recording laboratory are used to record music, literature, and auditory documentation. The Motion Picture, Broadcasting, and Recorded Sound Division administers all Library sound recordings.

Old age, poor workmanship, and rough handling—singly or collectively—can hasten the demise of a bound book, as in this example discovered by a Library worker.

PRESERVATION OFFICE

Public awareness of the very real possibility that library collections everywhere, printed on poor-quality paper and subject to environmental hazards, may not last for another hundred years, or even fifty, heightened interest in the Library of Congress preservation program during the late 1970s. The Library discovered in its own laboratory that distilled and deionized waters used for washing papers in restoration processes actually shortened the life of papers, as compared to those washed in tap water. This discovery startled the conservation community and caused the revision of many preservation operations.

The Library preserves and restores more than 250,000 volumes, rare books, and related materials annually. Microfilm conversions in 1979 included 4 million exposures of pages from brittle books and serials and almost 2 million exposures of newspapers and periodicals. In addition, the Preservation Office has averaged about 5,000 annual conversions from deteriorating sound disks to magnetic tapes.

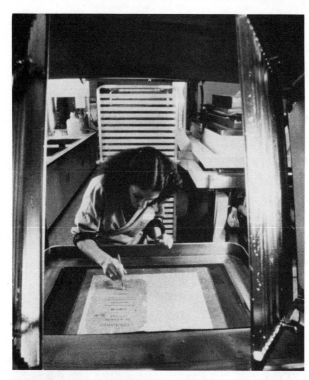

Individual pages that have deteriorated can be saved by special treatment with this leaf-casting machine.

Several tools and much patience are required to restore a book's binding.

The restoration of antique leather bindings is an ongoing function of the Preservation staff.

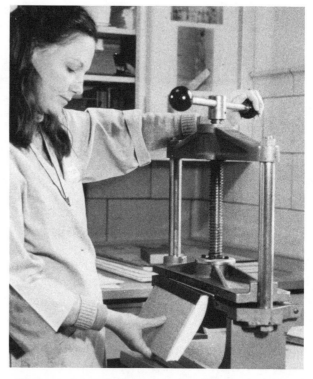

With its pages reassembled and its cover reconditioned, another book is given a new lease on life.

Because single sheets are reproduced more quickly and accurately than bound pages, this bindery employee is taking apart newspaper volumes that are to be photographed as part of the Library's program to preserve most of its newspaper files on microfilm.

Books whose pages have become too brittle for rebinding are transferred to microfilm. The films are then stored in boxes in a special stacks area in the Jefferson Building.

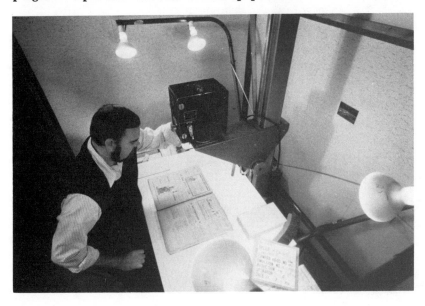

Microfilm photography helps preserve documents for future generations of researchers.

Continuing research at the Library helps find procedures to combat the natural processes of deterioration that affect the printed page. Results of such experiments as shown here are shared with librarians and conservationists in general.

Immersion in the solution of calcium bicarbonate and calcium hydroxide does not affect the legibility of the documents.

Thousands of valuable maps are laminated each year to protect them from the effects of handling.

After their alkaline bath, the manuscripts are laminated with cellulose acetate and tissue to ensure preservation.

Some maps are treated with sizing and placed in special folders.

Lamination also is used to protect documents, particularly single sheets.

Stiff backing and specially constructed boxes, binders, and portfolios protect the Library's prints and photographs.

Additions to the poster collection are mounted on muslin to protect them against damage.

4
USING MATERIALS
OF THE LIBRARY
OF CONGRESS:
SERIOUS RESEARCH

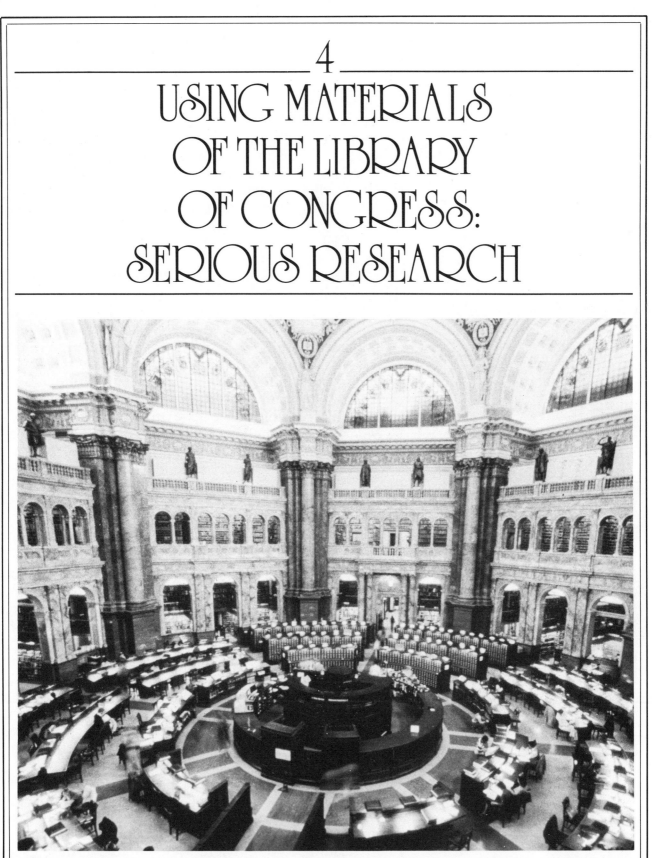

Inspiration certainly must fill the hearts and minds of people who study in the Library's Main Reading Room or Rotunda. The huge card catalog is located in the background with the attendants' area in the center. Three circles of desks can accommodate nearly 300 readers.

As its most important service to scholarship, the Library of Congress makes its vast resources—including over 2 million cataloged items—available to the general public. Scholars, writers, teachers, artists, journalists, students—anyone pursuing serious research—may use the facilities in its seventeen reading rooms, including card catalogs, computer terminals, reference collections, and librarians to guide the way. The computer terminals are tied into several data bases developed by the Library. Searchers for new titles, for sources of information on scientific subjects, and for legislative histories can take only a few minutes with the terminals.

The uses made of the Library's resources are as varied as its collections. For example, a graduate student doing a comparative study of American writers may go to the Manuscript Reading Room to examine the papers of Walt Whitman and Archibald MacLeish. A violinist may use the Music Reading Room to study the notations on an original score of a Mozart string quartet. A Spanish lawyer may go to the Law Library to use its comprehensive collection of foreign legal materials. A famous novelist may use the collections of the Main Reading Room, the European Division Reading Room, and the Newspaper and Current Periodical Room to prepare the background of a spy novel set in Eastern Europe.

Books from the general classified collections are available in the two general reading rooms—the Main Reading Room in the rotunda of the Thomas Jefferson Building and the Thomas Jefferson Reading Room on the fifth floor of the John Adams Building. In both rooms reference collections of frequently consulted works are directly accessible to readers; other books must be requested at issue desks. Books may be removed from the general classified collections; however, no one may remove books from the reference collections. A reader who needs a book for more than one day may reserve it for up to three days. The Library also has a limited number of special study desks and reserve shelves may be reserved for ninety days with renewal privileges. Researchers here may reserve books for the life of the assignment. The Library's Main Catalog is located in the Main Reading Room and an adjoining room to the east. The computer terminals are located in the entry to the Main Reading Room. There are computer terminals in the Thomas Jefferson Reading Room, but no card catalog. Reference assistants are available to help readers use the catalog and computer terminals, and to aid in locating materials.

Early in the morning, before the Library doors are opened to the public, the Main Reading Room is deserted—except for the ever-present statues above.

A newcomer to the Library receives an orientation briefing from a reference librarian in the Research Guidance Office.

Computer assistance is available at all hours when the general reading rooms are open. It is located at the Computer Catalog Center on the east wall of the Main Catalog area in the Main Reading Room. Information available via computer includes data on all books acquired by the Library since 1969, citations to journal articles having appeared since 1976 on topics relating to current events (an Automated Readers' Guide), and information on legislation introduced into Congress since 1973.

The special reading rooms have catalogs and terminals that supplement the general catalogs, and they are staffed by reference assistants who are experts in their subject fields. At the start of 1980, the Law Library, Microform, Music, European, Archive of Folk Song, Rare Book and Special Collections, and Hispanic reading rooms were located in the main building, as was the Congressional Reading Room, which is reserved for the use of members of Congress and their staffs. Located in the John Adams Building were the Newspaper and Current Periodical, Asian Division, Local History and Genealogy, Manuscript Division, Motion Picture, Prints and Photographs, Science, and African and Middle Eastern Division reading rooms. This last reading room is divided into three: African, Hebraic, and Near Eastern.

The two general reading rooms are open from 8:30 A.M. to 9:30 P.M. on weekdays (with stack service until 8:45 P.M.), from 8:30 A.M. to 5:00 P.M. on Saturday (with

Card trays may be removed to nearby tables for close study and for filling out call slips.

stack service until 4:00 P.M.), and from 1:00 to 5:00 P.M. on Sundays (with stack service until 4:15 P.M.). The hours of the special reading rooms vary, but the Law Library, the Science Room, the European Room, the Newspaper and Current Periodical Reading Room, and the Microform Room follow the same schedule as the general reading rooms.

As the James Madison Memorial Building was being occupied in stages during 1980, a number of reading rooms were being transferred to it. These included the Geography and Map, Congressional, and Law Library reading rooms.

SPECIAL LIBRARY SERVICES

For those who cannot come in person, the Library of Congress offers a number of special services. Through its interlibrary loan program, it extends the use of certain books and other materials to scholars working at academic and public libraries across the country. Junior college libraries and media centers are included in the definition of "academic" for loan purposes; other school libraries and media centers below that level are excluded.

Requests for such loans must come from the library concerned on standard American Library Association forms in accordance with the Interlibrary Loan Code. Forms should be addressed to: Library of Congress, Loan Division, Washington, D:C. 20540. Requests may also be submitted by teletype (710–822–0185) or, in cases of special urgency, by telephone (202–426–5444). If a teletype reply is desired, libraries should indicate on the message, "Please reply TWX collect." All requests will be handled as quickly as possible; those showing reply deadlines will be given special attention whenever possible.

In addition, the Library's Photoduplication Service enables the general public to purchase by mail—subject to copyright or other restrictions—photographs, photostats, facsimile prints, and microfilms of research materials. Written inquiries on specific subjects are routinely handled by the General Reading Rooms Division and other reference divisions.

These and other information aids are available for both new and experienced Library users.

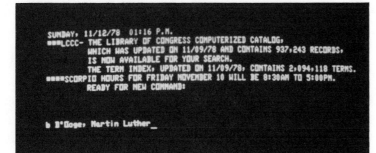

Computerized catalog assistance also is available through terminals in the entry to the Main Reading Room, as indicated on this computer screen, and in the Thomas Jefferson Reading Room.

Readers type requests for research sources that appear on television-like display screens. This is the computer catalog center of the Main Reading Room.

The main catalog in the Jefferson Building's Main Reading Room contains data on more than 2 million items for public use.

Foreign readers also use the card catalog for serious research.

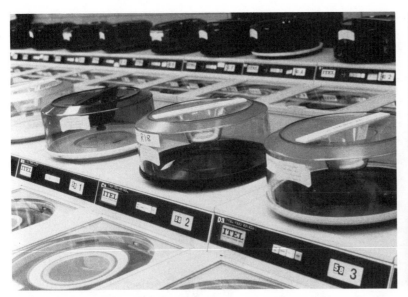

Banks of computer machinery store the millions of bits of data that Library readers call up when they request information from the terminals.

Elsewhere in the Library, a staff member also uses her computer terminal to search for information.

Information generated by computers can be displayed on electronic tubes or typed automatically on paper. Here an employee adjusts a printer in the Library's computer facility.

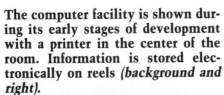

The computer facility is shown during its early stages of development with a printer in the center of the room. Information is stored electronically on reels *(background and right)*.

Having determined what books she needs, a reader turns in her call slips.

A desk attendant then pulls books from shelves in response to the reader's requests.

For decades call slips were rushed to the stacks through pneumatic tubes, as illustrated here. That system has been replaced by computer terminals.

The requested books are placed in a box and moved through a conveyer system to the Main Reading Room for the reader's use.

Similar issue procedures are followed in the Thomas Jefferson Reading Room at the Adams Building.

The Jefferson Reading Room is located on the fifth floor of the Adams Building. It is of traditional design and arrangement.

Young King Faisal II of Iraq examines a manuscript that was delivered to him in 1952 from the stacks by the large pneumatic tube *(right foreground)*. It was used between buildings from 1939 to 1978, when the book carrier system was replaced by a mechanical conveyer system.

Special study desks are available for scholars engaged in extensive research.

Readers may request the use of private study carrels in the main building.

Reading rooms are located in each of the three Library buildings on Capitol Hill. This gentleman is studying in the Science Reading Room at the Adams Building.

City directories from throughout the United States are included in the reference collection in the Main Reading Room.

A reference librarian examines a book in the stacks to help ensure that a reader obtains the most relevant sources.

A Microfilm Reading Room makes the Library's microfilmed books readily available.

A reader in the Main Reading Room is aided by a librarian from Information and Reference Assistance.

Desk attendants also check the shelves regularly to make sure that all books are in the correct place according to their call numbers.

This student finds it easy to concentrate on his research project.

These books in a reader's carrel were used for a study on clowns.

Readers customarily space themselves throughout the Rotunda to achieve a sense of privacy.

Many readers find it most convenient to work in the Main Reading Room.

The reference librarian is there to assist readers.

The Local History and Genealogy Reading Room, located in the Adams Building, is the mecca for many people tracing family histories. Biographical index files are one of the research sources.

Library staff members and other persons on the borrowers' list are eligible to check out books through the Loan Division of Research Services in the main building.

As the sign suggests, this reader is using the family name indexes.

Information on coats of arms also is available through the card catalog.

5
FOUNDATION FOR LAWS: CONGRESSIONAL RESEARCH SERVICE

A legislative aide from the Capitol *(background)* **arrives at the Library to use its research facilities.**

The Congressional Research Service works exclusively for Congress, conducting research, analyzing legislation, and providing information at the request of committees, members, and their staffs. The service makes such research available—without partisan bias—in many forms, including studies, reports, compilations, digests, and background briefings. Upon request, the service assists committees in analyzing legislative proposals and issues and in assessing the possible effects of these proposals and their alternatives. The service's senior specialists and subject analysts are also available for personal consultations in their respective fields of expertise.

Like every other legislative body in the world, the United States Congress frets over its inability to secure the information it needs to govern wisely. Its members know the distress of all legislators over the increasing number of decisions to be made, each concerning matters of the utmost complexity and usually involving highly technical, intricately related courses of action. Congress cannot hope to match the superior number of specialists available to the President and the executive departments, but it does attempt to equal them in the quality of the expertise that it builds into its congressional offices and committee staffs, and into its Congressional Research Service at the Library of Congress.

The Congressional Research Service, known as CRS in the congressional establishment, was founded in 1914 and has since grown steadily in staff and in the demands Congress has made upon it. In a recent fiscal year, the service responded to more than 313,000 congressional inquiries. The answers were provided by its 542 research specialists, supported by an additional 314 clerical and administrative personnel. An inquiry may be as simple as a question on the population of California or as complex as a study of the possible ways to provide medical care to the aged. The one required a few seconds by a researcher; the other occupied three analysts for a period of six months.

The development of such a research organization goes back to 1800, when Congress created a small working library to assist itself in governing the nation. The Library grew in scope through the years until its collections became so great they were, in fact, The National Library, and by the early 1900s the Library staff had become so involved in the complexities of operating a general research institution that Congress felt the need for a special department of the Library that would concentrate solely on matters of legislative interest.

Books, magazines, and documents on many subjects of legislative interest are available for study in the reading room. The fireplace is of Sienna marble with the sculpture panel of the same material by Herbert Adams.

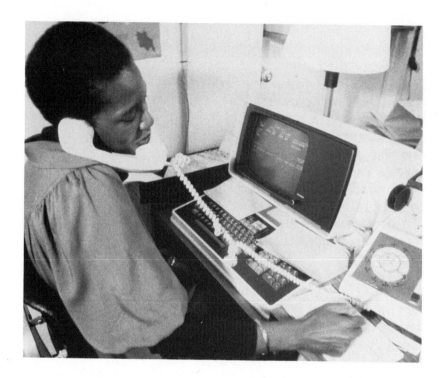

Requests for information from Capitol Hill are routed automatically to one of sixteen inquiry recorders.

Through the years of trial and error, plus the ever-present need for more and more specialized knowledge, the service has reached its present form of organization. It now attempts to house a diversity of subject specialists who match the spectrum of congressional needs. Its professionals are all college graduates, the majority with advanced degrees. Some feeling of the scope of the expertise available can be seen in the method by which an inquiry is assigned to one of the seven subject divisions of the service.

When a request or query is made of the CRS, the staff of its Inquiry Recording Unit first asks the questions, "Is this of such nature that the answer is purely factual? Will it appear in a book, in a previously prepared CRS report, or in one of the service's information files?" If so, the inquiry is sent to the Congressional Reference Division, where a group of sixty-four reference and information specialists will respond to it. Working from a typical public library reference collection and the service's materials on national affairs, this division handles more than 192,000 inquiries a year. Fifty percent of these are answered either "while the asker waits" or during the day of their receipt; the balance are answered within twenty-four hours.

SEVEN RESEARCH DIVISIONS

If the inquiry is of such a nature that it will require the preparation of a report, the projection of statistics, the analysis of the pros and cons of an issue, or any subject-oriented research, it will be sent to one of the research divisions below.

The American Law Division has forty-seven staff attorneys who deal with the legal aspects of all public policy issues, with special expertise in such fields as election law, international law, tax law, conflicts of interest, congressional ethics, civil rights, Indian law, environmental law, antitrust, criminal law, parliamentary law, administrative law, and the rights, privileges, and immunities of members of Congress. The division also prepares such continuing publications as the *Digest of Public General Bills*, the *Federal-State Election Law Survey*, and the *Constitution of the United States, Analysis and Interpretation*.

The staff of the Economics Division includes fifty-eight researchers whose skills and background cover the fields of money and banking, international trade, industrial organization, labor, communications, housing, urban development, transportation, and commerce.

The Education and Public Welfare Division's fifty-four researchers serve in the fields of Social Security, public health, crime, immigration, veterans' affairs, welfare, and education.

The Environmental and Natural Resources Policy Division has thirty-six professionals and is concerned with the governmental role in water resources, agriculture, mining, forestry, energy resources, oceans, and air and water pollution.

The Foreign Affairs and National Defense Division has fifty-six research staff members arranged in a miniature State Department of "desks"—for instance, Western European, Latin American, and Southeast Asian—with separate sections for regional issues, global issues, and policy management issues.

The Government Division, with fifty-three research employees, is divided into six principal sections: One provides information on Congress; the second deals with executive branch organization and administration; the third covers government operations and personnel; the fourth pursues research in the areas of civil rights and equal opportunity; the fifth responds to inquiries

Several hundred books are available for immediate reference in the Congressional Reading Room.

Reference librarians, such as this gentleman, are posted in the reading room to assist researchers from the nearby Senate and House office buildings.

Working conditions were a bit crowded when the Congressional Reference Division was located in the Jefferson Building. Nevertheless, researchers were able to answer most questions the day they were asked. The division now is in the new Madison Building.

A researcher tracks down the answer to one of the 2,000 inquiries placed during a typical legislative day.

concerning politics, history, and territories; and the sixth is concerned with planning, development, and survey research.

The Science Policy Research Division aids Congress in the evaluation of federal programs relating to space, atomic energy, oceanography, computer technology, research in medicine and the life sciences, and government support of scientific development and professional education. The division has thirty-three scientists on its staff.

In addition, the Language Services Section of the Office of Assignment, Reference, and Special Services provides foreign language translations to the Congress (1,500 translations in 1979 involving nineteen different languages).

SENIOR SPECIALIST POSITIONS

Finally, distributed throughout the service are the senior specialist positions. Their role and subject specialization are described by statute, and the positions are filled with nationally recognized experts. As a rule, they have published widely and have had extensive careers outside the CRS—in government, on the campus, or in private business. Frequently their experience has been in all three areas. The senior specialists' positions cover the fields of agriculture, American government and public administration, American public law, conservation and energy, education, engineering and public works, environmental policy, futures, housing, income maintenance, international affairs, international economics, labor, life sciences, mineral and regulatory economics, national defense, ocean policy, price economics, public administration, science and technology, social welfare, Soviet affairs, Soviet economics, space and transportation technology, taxation and fiscal policy, and transportation.

With the exception of the senior specialists, each subject division is organized in a comparable manner. At the top is the chief of the division, who is both a senior analyst with a broad experience background in the field of the division's responsibility—such as a general economist—and a specialist in some particular aspect of the division's work—such as an expert in corporate finance.

The chief is supported by an assistant chief (who is skilled in one of the division's subject specialties), an administrative secretary, and six to ten typists.

Within each division's specialized staff are vertical responsibilities. For example, in the field of housing, the service has five persons. The housing senior specialist prepares the highest level of studies bearing on legislative problems, assists with committee hearings, and provides consultative service as requested. The others in the unit are housing economists with advanced professional degrees who provide specialized assistance. At peak workload in the spring, an apprentice or generalist in the field (probably only recently graduated with a baccalaureate degree) frequently is added on a temporary basis to handle the less sophisticated requests. There are several units in each division, carrying the total divisional subject responsibility.

The Congressional Reading Room on the first floor of the main building is administered by the Congressional Research Service for the exclusive use of members of Congress, their staff assistants, and Library personnel.

FROM INQUIRY TO ANSWER

A member of Congress or staff assistant making an inquiry of the CRS telephones a single number, which automatically places the call with one of sixteen full-time inquiry recorders. This person conducts the interview with the inquirer, determines what the question is, records the inquiry, and passes the request to the unit supervisor, the coordinator of research. The coordinator, on the basis of the subject involved, the known workload of the divisions, the expertise of the personnel available, etc., assigns the request to a specific subject division, reviews assignments, and deals with crises.

The appropriate division chief then considers the skills and workload of that division's staff, and assigns the inquiry to a researcher. The researcher answers the inquiry using techniques to be explained below, and returns the reply to the chief. The chief approves or modifies the response, and the reply is sent to the congressional office. Thus, more than half of all CRS inquiries are answered within the day they are received. The service receives more than 2,000 calls a day during the legislative session.

Such speed and quantity does not imply a superficial response, but rather one that was anticipated. This is achieved by eliminating the majority of the usual steps in a research project: searching the literature on the subject and accumulating the material for the inquirer.

The Congressional Research Service attempts to minimize these labors through the use of its Library Services Division, made up of twenty-one professional librarians and fifty paraprofessional and clerical assistants. These specialists maintain a massive filing system in which all the past research of the service is arranged by subject and preserved, into which the contents of nine daily newspapers are classified and filed each day, and in which 4,000 magazines are clipped and filed as cuttings. This content, with the addition of enormous quantities of documents and pamphlets from the nation's governmental and lobby presses, results in a system that brings together in a single area some 3,000 different subjects, each arranged chronologically and available for instant use. The specialist can then begin immediately on a summary or analysis, or—if the literature is sufficient in itself—can employ the various photocopying devices in the service to copy and forward the material to the member at once.

Analysts in the Foreign Affairs and National Defense Division use maps, graphs, and books to prepare a detailed response for a congressional committee.

Similarly, when a topic is arousing general legislative interest, one of the earliest inquiries received on the subject is answered with a summary of the problem, a description of past governmental activities and alternative solutions for the future. From 350 to 5,000 copies will be reproduced in anticipation of further inquiries.

A researcher may answer a congressional inquiry in a great number of ways, depending upon what is most appropriate to the subject matter and which will be most useful to the member.

The researcher may elect to reply to the question simply by telephoning the answer to the member, drawing on personal knowledge of the subject. The answer may be found in one of the Library of Congress's 18 million volumes and photocopied, abstracted, or loaned to the congressional office. A written report, analysis, or survey may be prepared or the factual portions of an address drafted. A kit of material from duplicate copies of reports, documents, or photocopied articles may be assembled. Or the researcher may go personally to the inquiring member or committee and consult with them on the matter.

REFERENCE TOOLS AID CONGRESS

In addition to such individually tailored replies, the service provides continuing tools that assist the members with the daily flow of legislation. It prepares a

When congressmen on the floor or in committee meetings need reference books from the Library, a conveyer in this tunnel carries the books to the Capitol in about five minutes.

The conveyer terminates at the Library Station in the Capitol, where staff members forward the books to waiting senators or representatives.

Digest of Public General Bills, which identifies each new piece of legislation introduced in either house. The "Bill Digest" provides an abstract of each bill, keeps track of the status of its progress through Congress, maintains a list of bills by the names of the members who introduce them, and contains an index of the legislation by subject.

A second legislative aid, *Major Legislation of the Congress*, appears monthly and traces only the 600 to 700 most active pieces of legislation. It identifies committee activity, amendments, and the progress of these major bills and provides the public law number, when enacted.

Finally, the service sends each member a monthly list of the major studies done by the service, so that the congressional offices can know what has been newly prepared and what is currently stockpiled in the CRS on major congressional issues. At any one time, over 1,000 such studies are in print and available.

SCOPE OF SUPPORT INCREASED BY LAWS

Since the World War I era, the mission and purpose of the service has progressed through three clear-cut stages. From 1914 to 1946, the then Legislative Reference Service (LRS) was essentially a library operation with a librarian staff, primarily committed to the location and transmittal of data-reference work. This was used increasingly by the Congress and became an accepted source of legislative information support.

The enormous demands placed on government by World War II and the postwar reconstruction period demonstrated a congressional need for much greater subject expertise. Accordingly, in the Legislative Reorganization Act of 1946, additional staff with increased specialization was made available to members' personal staffs and given to the LRS. The LRS was instructed to act as a pool of experts, and brought together staff trained in specific areas that could be drawn on by both members and committees. The results of the 1946 act were to shift the predominant staff from librarians to subject specialists and to add pro and con studies, comparative analyses, and subject-oriented reports to continued information support.

Twenty years after the Legislative Reorganization Act, Congress again reexamined its informational needs, and in a new Legislative Reorganization Act of 1970 greatly enlarged the LRS's mandate and mission. During the hearings on the act and ultimately in the final report, it was made clear that the new instructions were based on three premises: (1) In order for Congress to sustain its constitutional role and maintain any kind of parity with the executive and judicial branches, it must have adequate information. (2) The information must come from a legislative source, detached, objective, and without a cause to sell. (3) Congress should have direct access to its own separate research agency, staffed with a pool of independent subject experts.

From this came an endorsement of the purpose and procedures developed under the 1946 act and four changes or extensions in previous instructions.

First, superficially trivial but representing the whole thrust of the new plan, the name Legislative Reference Service was changed to Congressional Research Service. "Legislative" could be state; "Congressional" was solely federal. "Reference" implied identifying it in stored material; "Research" implied bringing skilled thought to bear on the meaning of the information found. The requirements of in-depth policy analysis were spelled out.

Second, the new service's obligations to committees were underscored. Now, by law, the service was to maintain continuous liaison with all committee memberships and staffs. At the beginning of each new Congress it was to provide each committee with a list of all the programs and activities falling under each committee's jurisdiction that were due to expire during the coming sessions. Similarly, at the opening of each Congress, the service was to identify policy areas that each committee might profitably consider in the coming months. In so many words, the CRS was to assist committees with the analysis and evaluation of legislative proposals, to help them in determining the advisability of such proposals by "estimating the probable results . . . and of alternatives to them," and to evaluate "alternative methods of accomplishing the goals of such proposals."

Third, the service was instructed to prepare "purpose and effect reports" on any legislative measures that were scheduled for hearings. These were to be descriptions of "relevant measures . . . previously introduced in the Congress and a recitation of all action taken theretofore by or within the Congress" relative to the measure.

Fourth and finally, the act directed the Librarian of

Senator Claiborne Pell of Rhode Island receives an Issue Brief prepared by the Congressional Research Service.

The serial collection of congressional documents appears almost like an artistic creation of repeated patterns.

Issue Briefs are short reports that summarize specific legislation. The top two here are "Residential Applications of Solar Heating and Cooling Technology" and "Private Pension Reform."

Congress to "encourage and assist the service in performing its work, and to grant it complete research independence and the maximum administrative independence."

In general, the system works well, and the steady and growing demands made on the service attest to its usefulness to Congress. The service sees itself as the agent of Congress in securing and transmitting information—identifying truth to the best of its ability—from which the members make decisions. It endeavors to preserve its good name so that members of all parties can say on the floors of Congress, "The Congressional Research Service says . . ." and at least that part of the debate will meet with a minimum of challenge.*

* From a report by Charles A. Goodrum and Jane A. Lindley of the Library staff.

6
INTERNATIONAL IN SCOPE: THE LAW LIBRARY

Little storage space was required in 1832 when the Law Library opened with 2,011 books. In less than 150 years the total expanded to 1.6 million volumes, outgrowing this facility in the Jefferson Building.

While most congressional inquiries go to the Legislative Reference Service, another Library of Congress department, the Law Library, supplies a great deal of information to individual members of Congress and congressional committees from its 1.6 million-volume collection of works covering the laws of every age and country.

The Law Library became a separate department of the Library of Congress in 1832, when 2,011 law books, including 639 from Thomas Jefferson's library, were placed in a special room in the Capitol. For many years the chief justice of the Supreme Court chose the works that were added to the collection and, with the associate justices, made the rules governing their use. The justices could not prohibit the use of the collection by the President, the Vice President, and members of Congress, but otherwise they ran the Library. Today, the Law Library operates under the overall direction of the Librarian of Congress and the immediate supervision of the Law Librarian, who directs a staff of eighty-four experts in United States law and foreign law. In addition to the Law Library in the James Madison Memorial Building, which is open to the general public, there is a branch library in the Capitol for the exclusive use of Congress.

In both its organization and its staff, the Law Library reflects the international interests and responsibilities of the United States. Its American-British Law Division works with the laws of the United States, Australia, Canada, Great Britain, India, New Zealand, Pakistan, certain other countries of the British Commonwealth and their dependent territories, and Eire. The Library's Hispanic Law Division includes Spain, Portugal, Latin America, the Philippines, Puerto Rico, and Spanish- and Portuguese-language states of Africa. The European Law Division deals with the laws of continental European countries other than Spain and Portugal.

China, Japan, Korea, Thailand, Indonesia, and the former British and French possessions in the area are the responsibility of the Far Eastern Law Division. The Near Eastern and African Law Division works with the laws of those parts of the world, including the Arab states, Turkey, Iran, and Afghanistan, and all African countries, except Spanish- and Portuguese-language states and possessions.

The Law Library's primary responsibility is to provide to Congress reference and research service in the areas of foreign, international, and comparative law, and reference service in American law. In addition, the Law

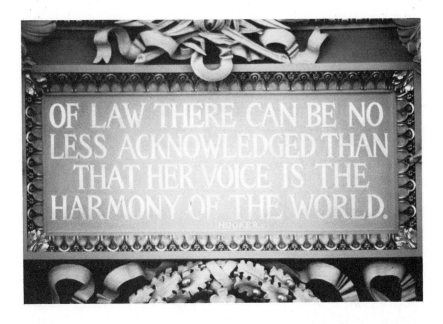

The great domed reading room in the main building contains eight statues representing the eight characteristic features of civilized life and thought. This inscription is over the statue of Law.

Library provides reference and research assistance to the executive and judicial branches of government, research organizations, members of the bench and bar, and others concerned with legal scholarship. Most of the Law Library's work demands not only a thorough familiarity with bibliographic services and the techniques of legal research, but also a knowledge of foreign languages and of foreign and international law. For the most part, members of the reference and research staff have been trained as lawyers in their native countries, and many have acquired American law degrees. Their linguistic competence covers nearly fifty languages.

Two major reference facilities and three foreign-law rare-book reading areas are maintained by the Law Library for general use. Patrons of these facilities benefit from the expert assistance of the reference and research staff and gain access to all of the materials in the law collection.

The Anglo-American Law Reading Room boasts a 33,000-volume American and British reference collection and seating for 125 readers. This collection includes sets of federal and state statutory and administrative materials, court reports, digests, law reviews, loose-leaf services, treatises, and other important secondary sources and finding aids. The Law Library's collection of U.S. Supreme Court and courts of appeals records and briefs are also serviced through this reading room. Adjacent to the reading room is the microform facility, which includes two microfilm readers, a microfilm-microfiche reader-printer, a microfiche reader, and an opaque card reader. Most of the legal materials on

Before the Madison Building was occupied, members of the Law Library located in the main building had to move desks and chairs to reach certain reference books. Overcrowding had forced use of some stacks as office space.

Among the publications received by the Far Eastern Law Division is the Constituent Assembly of Thailand's *Proceedings.* This is the title page of volume 3.

microform—6,000 reels of microfilm and 120,000 microfiche—are housed here. Also in this area is a coin-operated copying machine.

The Law Library's collection of U.S. legislative documents is maintained in the gallery surrounding the Main Reading Room. Over 30,000 volumes of House and Senate publications—the *Congressional Record* (and its predecessors), the serial set, and an almost complete set of bills and resolutions—are available for use. Current documents, committee prints, reports, and hearings also can be consulted.

Limited reference and research service is available to those who are unable to come in person to the Law Library. Such service includes brief (similar to a legal brief) responses to specific American, foreign, international, and comparative law inquiries, and providing bibliographic information and guidance. It also includes giving limited linguistic assistance in the fifty foreign languages handled by the research staff and making available on a selective basis research studies prepared by the staff and cleared for general distribution.

The Law Library is also able to facilitate legal research through the preparation and publication of bibliographical aids. Important among these are the subject indexes to 60 of the 270 official gazettes received in the Law Library and the annotated guides to the law and legal literature of various foreign countries.

Materials in the law collections that are not available locally or regionally may be obtained by interlibrary loan through a municipal, county, state, college, university, or bar association library. Correspondence concerning interlibrary loan should be addressed to the Chief of the Loan Division, Library of Congress. Many of the items that cannot be provided through interlibrary loan may be photocopied. Requests for photoduplication should be addressed to the Chief of the Photoduplication Service.

Attorneys and students use the research facilities of the Law Library's Reading Room. The extensive resources include microfilm and microfiche, as well as books and other printed documents.

These rare old law books from a number of countries are part of the Law Library's million-volume collection.

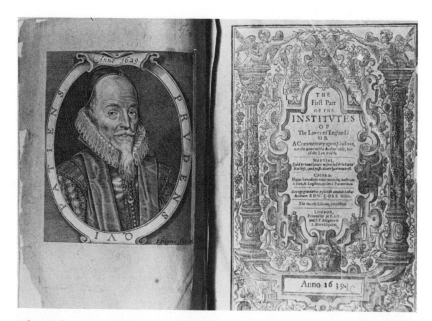

Members of Congress and others interested in Laos can consult a copy of that country's former constitution in the Law Library.

The title page *(right)* of part I of the third section of Sir Edward Coke's *The Institutes of the Law of England.* Printed in 1639, it is one of the most important of the early legal works in the Law Library.

"Costumes de Normandie," painted between 1450 and 1470, contains this miniature courtroom scene that is now in the Law Library.

THE
SACCO-
VANZETTI
CASE

TRIAL
OF
AARON BURR

These titles are just a sampling of the vast collection of books in the Law Library.

POLAND

ORZECZNICTWO
SADOW I
KOMISJI ARBITR

POLAND

ORZECZNICTWO
SADOW I
KOMISJI
ARBITR.

POLAND

ORZECZNICTWO
SADOW I
KOMISJI
ARBITR.

7
A MILLION ITEMS A YEAR: PROCESSING SERVICES

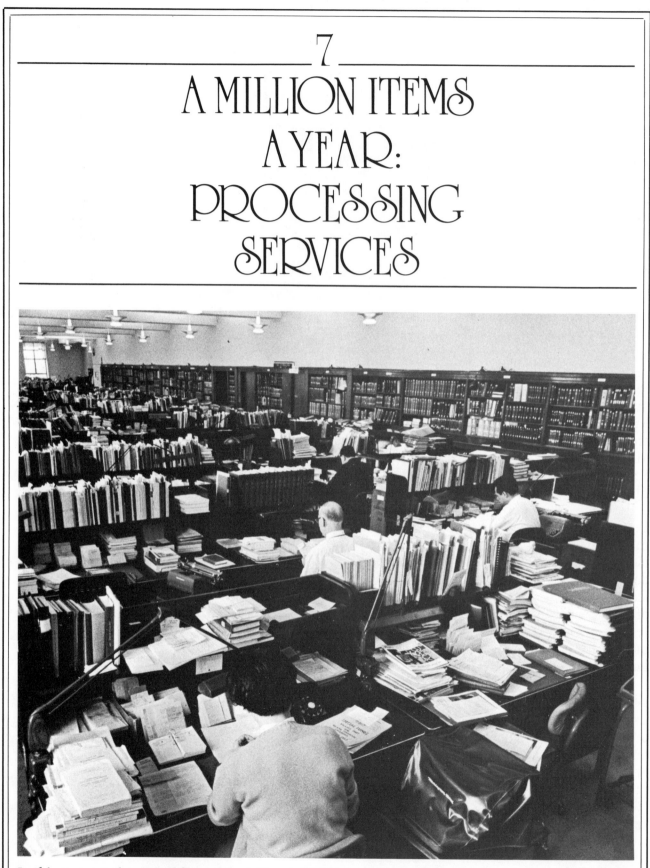

In this room on the second floor of the Jefferson Building catalogers determine how books will be listed in the Library's card catalogs.

In order to provide Congress, government agencies, and the general public with adequate service, the Library of Congress constantly adds to its collections. Information about new countries, new leaders, and new developments in every field of knowledge must quickly appear on its shelves and in its catalogs. At the same time there is a continuing effort to fill gaps in the collections. Over the past two decades approximately a million items, both old and new, have been added each year. The acquisition and preparation of this material is the responsibility of the Library's Processing Services department, whose 1,500-member staff is housed in all three Library buildings and, until August 1981, in temporary quarters in the nearby Navy Yard Annex on the Anacostia River.

As one of the many services it performs for libraries and other agencies, the Library of Congress also publishes lists of the new material it acquires. For example, the *Monthly Checklist of State Publications* lists documents received from official state and insular agencies. Russian publications received by the Library of Congress and a group of cooperating libraries are recorded in the *Monthly Index of Russian Accessions*. The annual *New Serial Titles* lists both new serial publications and libraries where they can be found.

Before books and other materials acquired by the Library of Congress can become useful additions, they must be assigned a definite place in its collections. This is done by the Library's catalogers, who prepare a precise description of the work, determine its subject or subjects, and assign it a classification number on the basis of its subject matter. Because the Library of Congress receives a high proportion of the world's publishing output, its catalogers must be familiar with many languages as well as with professional techniques.

The trend in much library work, as the twentieth century nears its close, is toward increased cooperation. Library budgets are tight and few libraries can afford to duplicate collections and services or embark on major automation projects without joining a cooperative program. Library patrons have greatly expanded their expectations concerning the information resources that libraries should be able to provide. If libraries are not to frustrate these expectations they must work together to meet them. The Library of Congress, as the national library and, in a sense, an example to the library community, continues to explore new areas of cooperation with libraries here and abroad to strengthen existing arrangements.

A Processing Services employee perforates a new work with the mark that identifies every Library of Congress book.

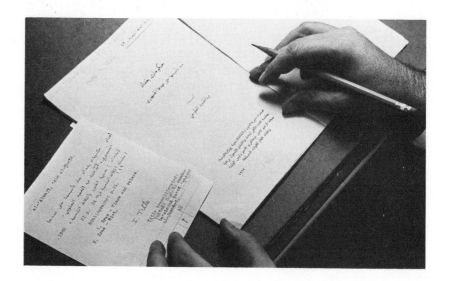

A cataloger compares a manuscript card for a book in Arabic with the book's title page to make sure the information on the card is accurate.

ACQUISITIONS

Acquisitions for the Library of Congress and other research libraries, using foreign currencies appropriated by Congress, are made in Cairo, which covers Egypt and other Middle Eastern countries; in New Delhi, which covers India, Nepal, Sri Lanka, Bangladesh, Burma, and Thailand; in Karachi, which covers both Pakistan and Afghanistan; and in Jakarta, Indonesia. The twenty-five libraries participating in the Cairo operation can contribute partial support to the program, but its continuation depends upon congressional willingness to appropriate dollars to fill the gap. A significant change in the program in 1978 was the production of microfiche by the New Delhi office. The Jakarta office selected 827 titles which were sent to New Delhi, microfiched, and distributed to participating libraries. Purchasing hard copies of these titles would have cost $11,456 for each library; microfiche copies were supplied at a cost of $1,855.

At shared cataloging centers, overseas publications are not only acquired but cataloged, thus shortening the time until they are available to research scholars in the United States. Cooperative exchange agreements continue to add to the Library's collections. The Library maintains over 13,000 exchange agreements with other institutions. There are 102 "official exchange" partners that receive either full or partial sets of U.S. official publications and give the Library comprehensive sets of publications in return. The other exchanges are with institutions whose wants and contributions are more limited and selective.

CATALOGING

The Library has been sharing cataloging information on printed cards with other libraries since 1901. This service required a tremendous inventory of all the cards ever printed and a considerable number of people to search and pull the orders. The last of the card inventory was discarded in September 1978 when the eagerly awaited Card Automated Reproduction Demand System (CARDS) became operational. This system—which uses laser, Xerographic, and computer technology to print cards on demand—shortens time in response to orders, eliminates the need for maintaining printed cards in stock, and thus produces significant savings in staff and space.

A more recent method of sharing cataloging information, Cataloging in Publication (CIP), increased its coverage of the total U.S. publication of book titles to 73 percent in 1978. Over 1,700 American publishers now send material to the Library in advance of publication so that the main elements that appear on a catalog card can be printed in the book itself, usually on the reverse of the title page. So useful has this program been to libraries, dealers, and book purchasers in the United States that similar programs have been started in other countries.

Before CIP, libraries could catalog books themselves or wait up to four months to receive printed catalog cards. In either case, books were delayed in reaching the shelves and readers. A library receiving a CIP book, on the other hand, has sufficient information to make its own catalog cards or to establish preliminary controls that make it possible to get books into circulation immediately. With CIP data, private purchasers of books, book dealers, and offices with book collections too small to warrant employment of a professional librarian can arrange their collections for easy and efficient use. Subscribers to machine-readable cataloging (MARC) tapes can use CIP information to order new books and to order Library of Congress catalog cards, and ideally the two will arrive at their destination at approximately the same time.

While librarians are saving time and effort in processing new books under the CIP program, they are saving money as well. When the cataloging and processing of a book are done entirely internally, costs can run to as much as twice the price of the book.

The U.S. Government Printing Office (GPO) and the Library coordinate cataloging produced by the Library

After examining a book and deciding what subject headings fit it best, a cataloger adds the headings to a card. A laser will be used to produce the final card.

During the cataloging process each book is assigned the Library of Congress classification number that corresponds to its subject, and, in many cases, a Dewey decimal classification number as well.

This cataloger examines a newly published book to determine what card catalog data should be transferred to the Card Automated Reproduction Demand System.

A former editor of the Classification Office works on changes in the Dewey decimal classification system, which is used by a large number of libraries. Both it and the Library of Congress classification system undergo constant revisions to keep them up to date.

with that done by the GPO Library for its *Monthly Catalog of U.S. Government Publications*. Another major cooperative undertaking involves the International Standard Serial Number (ISSN)—a unique identifying number assigned to magazines and other serial publications on a worldwide basis. The Library is responsible for assigning ISSNs to serial publications with a U.S. imprint. The U.S. Postal Service, which had required an identifying number for publications mailed at second-class rates, after consultation with Library officials now uses the ISSN as the official registration number. The Library staff assigns numbers to new and changed titles as they are received by the Postal Service for second-class registration.

NETWORKING

"Networking" is an idea that has demanded the attention of the library world ever since computers and machine-readable cataloging (MARC) made such a development possible. The Library of Congress, knowing that it cannot provide all the bibliographic records needed by the library community, has welcomed the idea of receiving records from other institutions and distributing them through networks to yet other libraries. To develop a standardized bibliographic basis for doing this, the Library drafted a document entitled *National Level Bibliographical Record—Books*, setting forth the bibliographic content needed to make a record in the machine-readable format acceptable as a national level record.

Library of Congress Cataloging in Publication Data

Hartman, Jane E
    Looking at lizards.

    Bibliography: p. 117
    Includes index.
    SUMMARY: Discusses the physical characteristics, habits, and environments of a variety of lizards and presents instructions for keeping lizards as pets.
    1. Lizards—Juvenile literature.   [1. Lizards. 2. Lizards as pets]   I. Title.
QL666.L2H35   598.1'12   78-5357
ISBN 0-8234-0330-0

The MARC data base, which is being used more and more frequently as a bibliographic source supplementing the card catalogs, contains bibliographic records of English-language books cataloged by the Library of Congress since 1968. Books cataloged by the Library in other Roman-alphabet languages have been phased in gradually since 1972.

The MARC data base offers the Library new ways to utilize its bibliographic resources. One of these ways is use of the information retrieval program, the MARC Retriever. The Retriever is able to produce bibliographic listings by making available any data found on the catalog card, plus many additional elements which have been specifically coded in the machine record—such as biographies, translations, language of text, directories. Although some searches are more economically done using card or book catalogs (for instance, books by Theodore Roosevelt or books on skin diving), for more complex bibliographic needs, computer searching and printing can save enormous amounts of time and energy. The compilation of subject bibliographies, for example, may be simplified by combining several subject headings and Library of Congress class numbers in a single search.

Community librarians have had their work eased a bit by the Library of Congress through its Cataloging in Publication (CIP) procedure. Information as shown here is provided by the Library to publishers for printing on the reverse side of title pages. Upon receiving a new book, the local library can use the CIP data to prepare its catalog card.

Laser, Xerographic, and computer technology are used at the Library of Congress to print catalog cards on demand for files of local libraries.

Like any publisher, Processing Services is proud of its many catalogs in book form. Here two employees inspect one of the catalogs.

Left: This employee is packaging copies of the *National Union Catalog* for shipment to subscribers. Published in nine monthly, three quarterly, and annual cumulative issues, the catalog lists, by author, books acquired by the Library of Congress and other American libraries. *Right:* A book is almost ready for the shelves when a label carrying its classification number has been pasted in.

The processing department prepares its catalogs by mounting printed cards on boards *(foreground)*, which are then headed, paged, and marked for the printer. Its yearly output of mounted pages runs as high as 37,000.

Millions of cards, filed in the same order as books are arranged on the shelves, constitute the Library of Congress shelf list, the official record of the books owned by the Library.

Maintaining the general catalogs and special files in the Library keeps a staff of forty people busy. Each year they file over 1.5 million cards.

8
PROTECTION FOR THE AUTHOR: THE COPYRIGHT OFFICE

Printed materials submitted to the Copyright Office include newspapers from around the nation.

Applications arriving for copyright protection average about 1,400 each working day.

Most countries attempt to protect the rights of their authors, composers, and artists to the material they have created. In the United States, authors of books, maps, and charts have been protected against unauthorized copying since 1790, when the First Congress passed a law giving such authors the sole right to print, publish, and sell their copyrighted material.

Copyright registration was handled by a number of federal agencies until 1865, when a revision of the law stipulated that a printed copy of each copyrighted work must be deposited in the Library of Congress. Another revision in 1870 made the Librarian of Congress responsible for all copyrighted records and materials. During the nineteenth century, protection was gradually extended to include musical, dramatic, and artistic works. The resulting flood of applications for copyright kept Librarian Ainsworth Rand Spofford and his small staff very busy. Deposits from the public numbered 6,680 in 1869, 11,512 in 1870, and 19,826 in 1871—the first full year of copyright operations in the Library. By 1896, the year before the Library's move into the then new main building, registrations totalled 72,482. (The number of items deposited was much larger than registered.)

The Library of Congress got its first register of copyrights in 1897. A copyright law passed in 1909 gave the Copyright Office its name. Copyright protection has been extended to periodicals, motion pictures, videotape recordings for television, sound recording, electronic music, sermons, lectures, designs for jewelry, fabrics, and other useful articles, commercial prints and labels, directories, choreography, and—most recently—computer tapes.

Over the years the Copyright Office has registered a total of 17 million items; the current registration rate exceeds 410,000 annually, some 25 percent above 1972. Roughly 50 percent of the deposits that must accompany the registrations are transferred to the Processing Department for addition to Library of Congress collections or for distribution to other libraries as exchanges or gifts. The remaining 50 percent, which consists of such nonlibrary material as advertising brochures and textile designs, is retained by the Copyright Office for several years as a part of its records. Copyright fees deposited into the U.S. Treasury approach $4 million annually, and continued to climb at the end of the decade. The long-sought goal of currency in filing into the copyright card catalog became a reality in 1976 with the scanning, arranging, and filing of more than 1.38 million compu-

Jukeboxes must be licensed by the Copyright Office under terms of legislation enacted during the 1970s. "Works of art" such as these figures also are protected by copyright law.

ter-produced cards. In addition, a new service of providing subscribers with computer tapes of catalog entries was instituted.

The Copyright Office publishes a *Catalog of Copyright Entries* (available in major libraries) twice each year and *Decisions of the United States Courts Involving Copyright* every two years. Its *Copyright Enactments: Laws Passed in the United States since 1783* is in loose-leaf form.

The new copyright statute that became effective on January 1, 1978, superseding the Copyright Act of 1909, includes a number of significant innovations. Thus, instead of the old dual system of protecting works under the common law before publication and under the federal statute thereafter, the new law provides a single

A variety of table games.

This Columbia record label is typical of the many that are submitted for copyright protection.

unitary system of statutory protection for all copyrightable works, whether published or unpublished.

The term of copyright protection for works created on or after January 1, 1978, is equal to the life of the author plus an additional fifty years. The new term for works made for hire and for anonymous and pseudonymous works is seventy-five years from publication or one hundred years from creation, whichever is shorter. This same term is also generally applicable to unpublished works already in existence on January 1, 1978, that are not protected by statutory copyright and have not yet entered the public domain.

For works already under statutory protection prior to 1978, the new law retains the old term of copyright of twenty-eight years from first publication (or from registration in some cases), renewable by certain persons for a second period of protection, but increases the length of the second period from twenty-eight to forty-seven years. Copyrights subsisting in their second term at any time from December 31, 1976, through December 31, 1977, were automatically extended to last for a total term of seventy-five years from the date they were originally secured. However, copyrights in their first term on January 1, 1978, must still be renewed during the last year of the original copyright term to receive the full new maximum statutory duration of seventy-five years.

The judicial doctrine of "fair use," one of the most important and well-established limitations on the exclusive rights of copyright owners, receives express statutory recognition for the first time in the new law, which

Left: Staff members sort and route the daily avalanche of new materials. *Right:* A portion of the Copyright Office Accounting Unit, which handles the records of money received, fees refunded, fees turned over to the United States Treasury, and similar transactions.

Even blueprints of homes are received by the Copyright Office.

provides specific standards for determining whether particular uses fall within this category. In addition to the provisions for fair use, the new law also specifies conditions under which the making or distributing of single copies of works by libraries and archives for noncommercial purposes will not constitute an infringement of copyright.

The new law established an independent five-member agency in the legislative branch named the Copyright Royalty Tribunal. The limited compulsory license provisions of the old law were extended by the new act to include the payment of royalties for the secondary transmission of copyrighted works on cable antenna television (CATV) systems, the performance of copyrighted music in jukeboxes, and the noncommercial transmission by public broadcasters of published musical and graphic works. Retained in the new law, with some changes, are the provisions in the old law permitting compulsory licensing for the recording of music.

Registration in the Copyright Office under the new law is not a condition of copyright protection but is a prerequisite to an infringement suit. Subject to certain exceptions, the remedies of statutory damages and attorneys' fees will not be available for infringements occurring before registration. However, if a work has been published in the United States with notice of copyright, copies or phonorecords must be deposited in the Copyright Office for the collections of the Library of Congress, not as a condition of copyright protection, but rather under provisions of the law subjecting the copyright owner to certain penalties for failure to de-

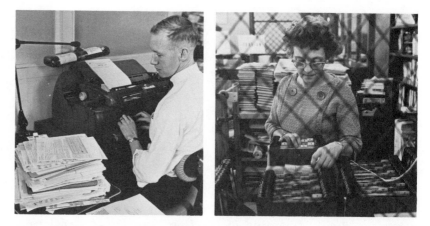

Left: **This staff member is filling out the control and accounting cards that help the Copyright Office keep track of the 410,000 deposits and nearly $3 million in fees received in the course of a year.** *Right:* **Copyright applications received ahead of deposit copies are filed until the books or other works arrive.**

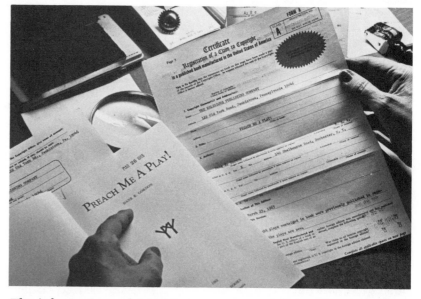

The information submitted on every copyright application undergoes a careful inspection. Prior to the Copyright Act of 1978, nineteen different forms were available. That total then was cut to only eight.

posit following written demand by the register of copyrights.

From 1969 to 1980, the Copyright Office was located at the Crystal City Mall in nearby Arlington, Virginia. With the completion of the James Madison Memorial Building, copyright functions were moved to the new structure. Public hours remain 8:00 A.M. to 4:00 P.M., Monday through Friday, except holidays.

A Copyright Office searcher consulting the 34-million-card catalog of copyright entries, which lists works by title, author, and copyright claimant. The catalog is open to the public; those unable to use the catalog in person can have an official search made by paying a nominal hourly search fee.

Sound recordings, whether disks or tapes, submitted to the Copyright Office are examined closely.

Many of the Copyright Office's 590 staff members work in large offices like this one.

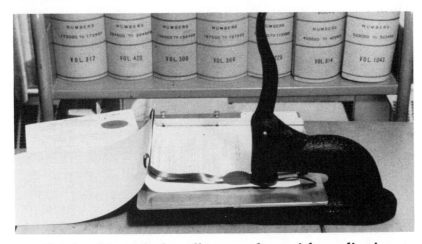

If a claim of copyright is in order, it receives an official registration number.

An official seal is applied to all approved copyright applications to protect the rights of the originator.

A selections officer determines which books deposited for copyright will be retained in the Library's permanent collection.

Millions of copyright catalog cards are available for reference, some dating back nearly two centuries.

More than 410,000 items annually are registered by the Copyright Office to protect the rights of authors, composers, and artists. Note the "Blondie" comic book at bottom left of the photograph in this temporary storage area.

The Copyright Office mails pamphlets explaining provisions of the copyright law to those who request information.

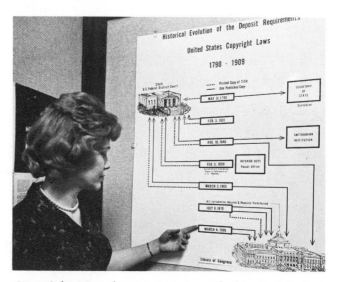

Copyright procedures were simplified by legislation enacted in 1909 and in 1978.

9
A UNIQUE GOVERNMENT AGENCY: NATIONAL PROGRAMS

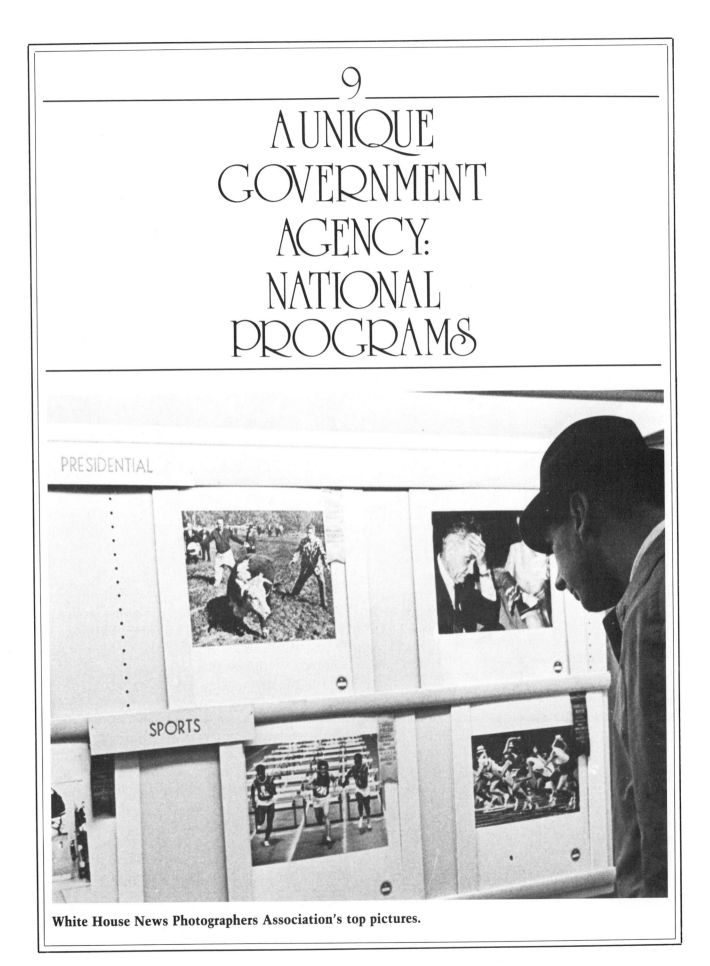

White House News Photographers Association's top pictures.

The Library of Congress—with its diverse collections that total in excess of 75 million items, its 5,400 staff members, and its astounding growth since its founding in 1800—would occupy a special place in the nation on the basis of size alone. But the Library of Congress has achieved its position of leadership also because of the many services it offers to the nation. Reference facilities for Congress, for other government agencies, and for the general public, books for the blind, the preservation of authentic American folk music and art, catalog cards, a long list of useful publications, sponsorship of literary and musical events, and copyright registration for creative works have placed the Library of Congress in direct or indirect contact with every citizen.

THE CENTER FOR THE BOOK

The Center for the Book in the Library of Congress was established by an act of Congress signed by President Jimmy Carter on October 13, 1977. Creation of the center is a dramatic example of the Library's desire to work closely with other organizations in the book community. The center's goal is to serve as an effective catalyst in the book world, stimulating interest in the book, exploring issues related to the crucial role of the printed word in the U.S. culture, and encouraging reading and research about books.

To carry out its mission, the center strives to bring together—in spirit and in action—authors, publishers, booksellers, librarians, educators, scholars, critics, and, above all, readers who are concerned about the role of the book in our society. The interests of the center include the educational and cultural role of the book; the history of books and printing; the future of the book; the international flow of books and the contribution of the book to international understanding; authorship and writing; publishing, design, and production of books; distribution, access, and use of books; reading; literacy; and the role and influence of the institutions of the book world.

In March 1978, more than sixty representatives of the book and educational communities met at the Library to discuss the center's potential activities and to establish

THE CENTER FOR THE BOOK
&
THE CHILDREN'S LITERATURE CENTER

presents

in observance of
National Children's Book Week 1978
a lecture by

JILL PATON WALSH

Coolidge Auditorium

These two centers of the Library serve as catalysts in the book world, in this case, hosting a noted guest lecturer.

its initial organizational structure. George C. McGhee, former assistant secretary of state and ambassador to Turkey and to the Federal Republic of Germany, was appointed by the Librarian to serve as chairman of the center's National Advisory Board and its executive committee. At its first meeting the committee agreed that the center will focus its activities on projects designed to carry out the general objectives of dramatizing the importance of the book and the printed word, strengthening the programs of other organizations in the book and educational communities, and clarifying unanswered questions and providing new information for interested segments of the book world.

During its first year the center sponsored several programs. Specialized, illustrated talks were given by Mirjam Foot of the British Library, who spoke about British and Continental bookbindings, and by book designer Adrian Wilson, who discussed his *Making of the Nuremberg Chronicle*. A two-day national seminar entitled "Television, the Book, and the Classroom" was co-sponsored by the center and the U.S. Office of Education.

THE AMERICAN FOLKLIFE CENTER

The American Folklife Center was created by Congress with passage of the American Folklife Preservation Act in 1976 to "preserve and present American folklife" through programs of research, documentation, archival preservation, live presentation, exhibition, publication, dissemination, training, and other activities involving the many folk cultural traditions of the United States.

The center is structured with a small core of versatile professionals who both carry out and oversee programs. In the brief period of the center's operation it has begun energetically to carry out its mandate with programs that provide coordination, assistance, and model projects for the field of American folklife. The center is under the general guidance of the Librarian of Congress and a board of trustees composed of members from federal agencies and private life who are widely recognized for their interest in American folk traditions and arts.

This Freedom quilt catches the attention of Mrs. Jimmy Carter and daughter, Amy, during their visit to the Library's American Folklife Center. Mrs. Carter is one of many First Ladies to have toured the main building.

"American folklife" means the traditional expressive culture shared within various groups in the United States: familial, ethnic, occupational, religious, regional. Expressive culture includes a wide range of creative and symbolic forms such as custom, belief, technical skill, language, literature, art, architecture, music, play, dance, drama, ritual, pageantry, and handicraft. Generally, these expressions are learned orally, by imitation, or in performance, and are maintained or perpetuated without formal instruction or institutional direction.

"To preserve and present American folklife," the key phrase in the public law that established the American Folklife Center, offers a stirring mandate for the development of programs that touch and illuminate the varieties of folk cultural traditions in the United States. Most of the projects of the center take place outside Washington. The center is, according to its legislation, neither a grant-giving agency nor simply an archive but rather an operating agency committed to an active, varied program for the preservation and presentation of American folklife.

The center's program has been arranged around three major goals for the field of folklife. These goals give focus to the program and help translate the center's mandate into a coherent plan of action.

Coordinative Leadership for the Field. This role includes coordination of folklife activities for the center's

national constituency; coordination within the federal government of folklife activities; and coordination of the folk cultural endeavors of the Library of Congress as a cultural institution. Conferences on special or timely subjects, and directories of folklife activities, are good examples of coordinative projects through which the center can bring new focus and attention to important aspects of American folklife.

Assistance to the Field. This represents the center's commitment to serve the field of American folklife by offering assistance to folklife projects in response to requests from local and state government agencies, organizations, communities, and educational institutions. The desire to foster and present American folklife at the community level is strong; what is often lacking is the know-how for locating and presenting local folk cultural resources in meaningful and effective ways. The center can provide the necessary help and guidance.

Model Projects in the Field. These are projects initiated by the center itself. The efforts under the "Model Projects" goal include research, publications and media dissemination, and live presentations and exhibits.

More than 100 employees and tourists were on hand when this lunchtime concert started on Neptune Plaza. However, most projects of the American Folklife Center occur outside of Washington.

Sponsored by the American Folklife Center, the Bluegrass Cardinals perform on Neptune Plaza in front of the main entrance to the Library.

The diverse folk cultural traditions of the country have, as the American Folklife Preservation Act says, "contributed greatly to the cultural richness of the Nation and . . . fostered a sense of individuality and identity among the American people." The American Folklife Center, through its programs to preserve and present American folklife, is dedicated to fostering that cultural richness.

Fifty years and thirty days after the Archive of Folk Song was founded as a part of the Music Division, the archive was transferred to the American Folklife Center in 1978. During that same year a recording, "Folk-Songs of America, the Robert Winslow Gordon Collection, 1922–1932," was issued by the Library in honor of the archive's fiftieth anniversary. The recording reflects the attempt of the archive's first director, Robert W. Gordon, to document the extent and variety of American folksong.

The selections of the album represent Gordon's major interests: the origins of folksong in America, the interplay between British and African traditions in the United States, and the influence of popular culture on folk culture. Through the hiss and crackle that ineradicably mark early field recordings, these songs and tunes speak of the Blue Ridge Mountains, the Georgia Tidewater, and the San Francisco waterfront. A highlight is a rendition of what is considered by many the first published ragtime song, "The Wagon," sung by its composer, Ben Harney. "Folk-Songs of America" was edited by Neil V. Rosenberg and Debora Kodish.

The center publishes a quarterly newsletter, available upon request. Publications are a major part of the center's purpose. Brochures, booklets, guides, and scholarly efforts are under way. A variety of items—greeting cards, small publications, and folk crafts—are available for purchase at the Library's information counter. The center is authorized to receive monetary gifts through the Elizabeth Hamer Kegan Fund.

THE PERFORMING ARTS LIBRARY

The Library of Congress co-sponsors the Performing Arts Library at the John F. Kennedy Center for the Performing Arts in Washington. The Performing Arts Library, which opened in 1979, combines the un-matched resources of the Library of Congress with the unique cultural position of the Kennedy Center in a common enterprise that serves the general public, the researcher, and the performers, designers, and musical artists working there. In this place the performing arts—music, dance, theater, film, and broadcasting—come together in a reference collection of 3,000 volumes; current periodicals on the performing arts; recordings on disk and tape; videotapes; and posters, programs, play-bills, and heralds, some of which come from the Kennedy Center archives.

There are also direct links to the Library of Congress and all it can offer. A video-display computer terminal provides quick access to its vast storehouse of information about recent books and about organizations and legislation concerned with the performing arts; and an audio link allows visitors to listen to sound recordings from its large collections.

The library is located in the John F. Kennedy Center on the Roof Terrace level at the east end of the North Gallery. Its immediate neighbors in the Kennedy Center are the Terrace Theater and the Musical Theater Laboratory. Together they form an interactive complex for ideas, performance, and innovation, and together they seek to foster new talent, new works, and new audiences.

The reading room, which accommodates forty-four persons, houses the reference collection, computer terminal, card catalog, listening table, microform reader-printer, and photocopying machine. There are also cases and panels for exhibits of items from the collections of the Library of Congress and the Kennedy Center. Next to the reading room are listening and viewing stations, staff offices, and a conference room. The conference room is available by appointment for group listening and viewing and for meetings and seminars.

The reference staff of the Performing Arts Library will assist visitors in using the resources at the Kennedy Center, the more extensive collections at the Library of Congress, or they can put the visitor in touch with other performing-arts collections in Washington and across the country.

Librarian of Congress L. Quincy Mumford escorts Mrs. John F. Kennedy into the Library for a 1961 evening performance of *The Importance of Being Oscar*, featuring Michael MacLiammóir. Since 1979, the Library has cosponsored the Performing Arts Library at the John F. Kennedy Center for the Performing Arts in Washington, D.C.

NATIONAL LIBRARY SERVICE FOR THE BLIND AND PHYSICALLY HANDICAPPED

There is a nationwide network of more than 160 cooperating libraries that annually provides Braille and talking books and magazines to more than half a million blind and physically handicapped persons. The National Library Service for the Blind and Physically Handicapped dates from 1897, when John Russell Young, then Librarian of Congress, at the suggestion of his wife organized a Department for the Blind. A reading room was ready to welcome its public three days after the Library of Congress opened its doors in November of that year. Here were assembled the 200 volumes in raised characters already in the collections, and writing slates, typewriting machines, and other devices for the use of the blind. The room was open daily from 9:00 A.M. to 4:00 P.M., and Mrs. Young organized a daily reading hour during which volunteers would read aloud from books not available in Braille. Musicales, to which local musicians contributed their services, were held on Wednesday afternoons. Congress ensured the growth of the collection of embossed books by stipulating in 1913 that the American Printing House for the Blind at Louisville, Kentucky, which received an annual appropriation from Congress, should deposit in the Library of Congress one copy of each book manufactured.

The national service, which the Library now administers through cooperating libraries, began with the passage of the Pratt-Smoot Act of March 3, 1931. This act established a centralized national free library service for adult blind readers. Service was at first limited to the provision of books in Braille, but the program was enlarged in 1934 to include "talking books" (books and magazines on unbreakable microgroove records). A national lending library of Braille musical scores was established by legislation passed in 1962. The Pratt-Smoot Act was amended in 1952 to permit service to children as well as to the adults named in the original legislation, and a 1966 amendment extended national books-for-the-blind service to all persons who are unable to read conventional printed materials because of physical or visual limitations.

Visually impaired visitors regularly use facilities of the Library of Congress. Their first reading room in the main building dates back to 1897.

Thomas A. Edison, as early as 1878, had predicted the use of "phonographic books, which will speak to blind people without effort on their part," but for a long time the only recordings available were 78 rpm, with a playing time of about five minutes each. Seventy-two of them were needed to record a book that took twelve hours to read. The American Foundation for the Blind developed a 33⅓ rpm record, which it then manufactured. Beginning in 1934, the Library of Congress distributed these talking books to a greatly expanded audience of blind readers—fourteen years before commercial long-playing records were offered to the general public. People who lose their sight as adults find Braille most difficult to master. Eighty-five percent of the blind people in the United States are not sufficiently proficient in Braille to enjoy reading, according to the American Foundation for the Blind.

Fiction, nonfiction, and periodicals are now recorded at 8⅓ rpm, a compressed format which makes it possible to provide almost twice as much material as the 16 rpm records recently used and almost four times as much as the first long-playing records. Recording on magnetic tape has made possible the distribution of small cassettes, especially to students and mobile blind persons. Cassette books are recorded at 15/16 ips. New technology indicates the possibility of bringing projected books to a wider audience. Automation is already being used for the production of books and music. Special devices that allow the partially paralyzed or immobile patient to make use of phonographs and records are

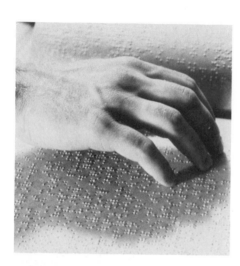

Braille characters are made of raised dots, read by the blind with their fingertips. One dot represents the letter "a" or the numeral "one."

available, with similar adaptations being produced for cassette machines.

Inability to utilize ordinary print because of any physical impairment establishes a person's eligibility for the program. A resident of the United States or one of its possessions, or a citizen of the United States living abroad, can have his disability certified by a physician, social worker, nurse, or therapist, and apply to the National Library Service for the Blind and Physically Handicapped, Library of Congress, Washington, D.C. 20542. There are more than 500,000 people enrolled in this program.

About 2,500 titles—Braille, talking books, and cassettes—are selected for production each year. These are professionally produced by the American Printing House for the Blind and the American Foundation for the Blind. Many more are produced by volunteers in religious and community-service organizations who braille or tape individual titles needed by blind readers. Titles to be made available throughout the network of libraries are being recorded in a national automated bibliographic service for which planning funds became available in 1973. In addition, *Talking Book Topics*, a bimonthly publication of the National Library Service, lists new titles that may be ordered through regional libraries. The listing is available in print and on records.

Phonograph players and cassette machines are available for free loan through cooperating network libraries. In a recent year the National Library Service shipped more than 1.8 million copies of 2,016 books and 878 magazines to network libraries for use by their patrons. Magazines offered for the first time in 1978 included the *New York Times* in recorded format and *Prevention*, *Outdoor Life*, and *Money* on disks.

A new building for the District of Columbia Public Library enabled that institution in 1973 to provide library service to blind and physically handicapped readers of the metropolitan area of Washington, D.C. The Library of Congress, which had had a reading room for the blind since 1897 and a regional library for the District of Columbia since 1931, trasnferred the regional library responsibility to this library at 1291 Taylor Street N.W., Washington, D.C. 20542. Reading materials are available to all readers through regional libraries. Music, however, is provided from the Library of Congress Annex on Taylor Street. Users of the music program have access to more than 40,000 volumes of musical instruction and a collection of music scores to which about 3,000 titles are added each year.

Braille magazines for a variety of tastes are distributed by the National Library Service for the Blind and Physically Handicapped.

Also available from the Library is a weekly edition of the *New York Times* in a large-type format. The weekly issue is recorded for those who have lost all vision.

Publications for the blind are issued in both large-type and Braille editions. Here, a staff member examines a catalog in Braille of books produced in Braille.

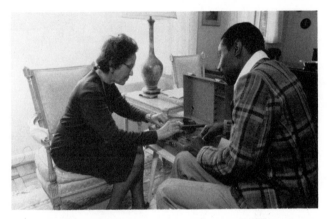

A representative from the Martin Luther King Library in Washington, D.C., explains the use of a phonograph machine to a visually impaired resident. The Library of Congress first issued recordings of books in 1934.

Two blind brothers in Maryland read a Braille book borrowed from their library. The Library of Congress directs a national program to provide Braille and talking books through 160 libraries.

Above: The Children's Literature Center, founded in 1963, answers about 3,000 questions a year. *Right:* Two visitors are shown an addition to the Children's Literature Center, which is used by illustrators, writers, publishers, and others.

CHILDREN'S LITERATURE CENTER

The Children's Literature Center, formerly the Children's Book Section, joined the Office of the Assistant Librarian for National Programs in June 1978 (from the defunct Reader Services Department). This new affiliation links the center to other unique programs of the Library that provide national leadership in specialized areas.

Since its founding in 1963, the center has served the research needs of those who study children's literature. Its clientele includes the creators of children's books—authors, illustrators, and publishers—as well as students and teachers of children's literature. In recent years they have averaged about 3,000 questions annually. Queries range from information about the McLoughlin picture books to questions about comic books. Following publication of the center's two Bicentennial works, *Americana in Children's Books* and *Children's Readings in America, 1776*, there was a significant increase in questions from historians and antiquarian bibliographers. Use of the center's resources and services are stimulated also by the release of supplements to its *Children's Literature: A Guide to Reference Sources.*

The Gutenberg Bible

Knowledgeable guides conduct adults and children on tours of the Library. They start on the hour in the basement of the main building.

TOURS AND EXHIBITS

More than 75,000 visitors to the Library of Congress are escorted on tours of the facility during a typical year. Three quarters of the guests participate in the regular tours while the remainder are visitors who have made special arrangements in advance. Professional visitors from the United States and abroad are included in the latter group. The regular tours start on the hour in the lower foyer (basement) of the Thomas Jefferson Building, preceded by a fifteen-minute multimedia presentation on the history and mission of the Library. Additional information concerning tours is available from the Information Office and, in the case of professional visitors, from the Education Liaison Office. Many visitors browse through the Library's gift shop while waiting for the hourly tours to begin.

Through the imaginative display of particularly significant items, exhibits also play an important role in communicating the breadth and scope of the Library's resources. Drawing on these resources, the Exhibit Office arranges for displays within the Library's buildings, lends displays to other institutions, and circulates them through a number of cities. One of the most publicized exhibits, because of the interest generated by the movie *Jaws*, was entitled "Sharks, the Marvelous Marauders." Others have included presidential campaigns, Charles Lindbergh, Babe Ruth's sixty home runs, the "100th Anniversary of the Birth of Carl Sandburg," and even "Arabic Calligraphy." When "China: Nineteenth-Century Drawings by Unknown Artists" was exhibited, additional information was solicited from the public about the artists and their works.

Responding to a witty remark from UPI photographer Stanley F. Stearns, Mrs. Richard M. Nixon and Librarian L. Quincy Mumford are snapped with big smiles. The occasion was the opening of the Twenty-sixth Annual News Photo Exhibit in 1969.

PHOTODUPLICATION SERVICE

Through its Photoduplication Service the Library of Congress can send copies of many of its materials to other libraries and agencies and to individuals. Started with a grant from the Rockefeller Foundation in 1938, the Photoduplication Service supplies microfilmed newspapers to 1,000 libraries and reproduces pictorial material, articles, and whole books in response to orders from all over the country.

Carrying out such a wide variety of services places heavy demands upon the Librarian of Congress, who must assemble a highly specialized staff, supervise the overall management of the Library, manage funds in excess of $185 million annually (mostly from Congress, but including some $15 million from gifts and other sources), and serve on numerous boards and committees as well. It also requires a dedicated staff and the support of members of Congress, whose appropriations have made the Library possible. And in the last analysis, the continued growth of the Library depends on an enlightened citizenry that realizes the value of its services.

Although it was established as a limited legislative reference library, the Library of Congress has become a great national institution whose resources provide essential services, not only to members of Congress but also to all government agencies and to industry, research institutions, other libraries, and scholars from every land. By keeping pace with the growing need for information of all kinds, the Library of Congress serves every citizen of the United States.

Special displays are arranged in connection with historical events and visits of dignitaries. This area is on the second floor of the Jefferson Building.

Another Library exhibit area is in the foyer on the fifth floor of the Adams Building.

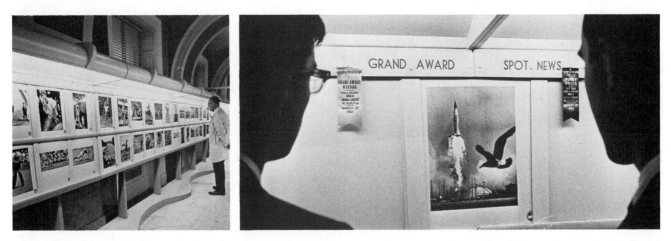

One of the most popular Library of Congress exhibits is its display each spring of the White House News Photographers Association's top pictures of the previous year.

A very popular exhibit with the younger generation was this special display showing animated cartoons, which began to appear in large number around 1914.

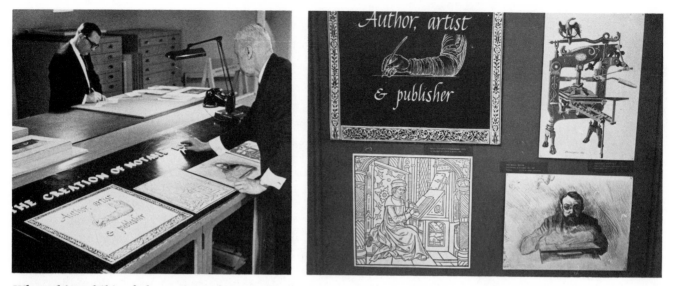

When this exhibit of the various elements in the creation of notable books was finished, it was displayed on the first floor of the Library's main building.

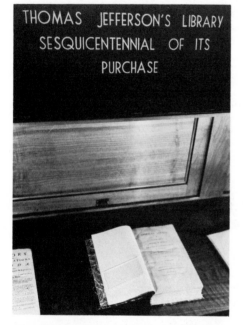

Poet St. John Perse loaned the Exhibits Office the original of an illustration in his *L'Ordre des Oiseaux*. Both it and the watercolor by Georges Braque *(right)* were featured in a Library display.

To commemorate the one hundred fiftieth anniversary of the purchase of Thomas Jefferson's personal library, the Library of Congress displayed fifty of his books in the Rare Book Room.

President Eisenhower visited the Library on several occasions in the 1950s. When he signed the guest book on March 31, 1954, he noted that it was his "grandson's 6th birthday." The President's wife had signed in earlier that month.

"Atoms for Peace" was one of the attractions during the 1955 visit of President Dwight D. Eisenhower. Atomic pioneers are pictured on the right, including the gray-haired Albert Einstein in the second row from the top.

When Princess Irene *(center)* of Greece visited the Library in 1967, she was given a copy of the 1966 edition of *The Library of Congress,* displayed by Assistant Librarian, Mrs. Elizabeth E. Hamer. Others are Librarian L. Quincy Mumford *(left)* and John P. Owens of the State Department. The current edition is available through the Library's gift shop.

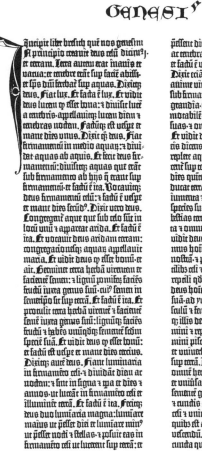

Above: Public tours start on the hour near the gift shop in the basement of the Jefferson Building where books, reproductions of Library holdings, and souvenirs are available. *Left:* Latin is the language used in the Gutenberg Bible, and this is the first page of Genesis as reproduced from the priceless copy displayed at the Library. An exact facsimile of the page in three colors, measuring about 11 by 15 inches, is available in the gift shop.

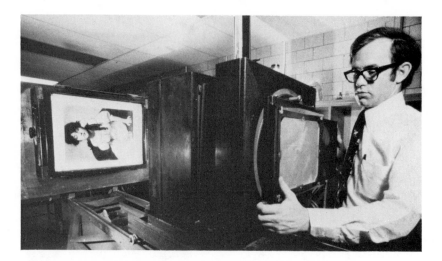

One picture or an entire book can be reproduced by the Library's Photo-duplication Service.

PRESS FIRMLY CALL NUMBER	PRESS FIRMLY PRESS FIRMLY AUTHOR .... BOOK/PERIODICAL TITLE	PERIODICAL VOLUME OR DATE

MAIN READING ROOM	Correct Legible Name and Address Required	**STAFF USE ONLY**
DESK NUMBER	NAME	Not on Shelf
		Clarify Call No.
	ADDRESS	Give Volume No.
If you have not indicated a desk number, do you wish this book for Hold Overnight ☐ Call ☐	CITY	Give Complete Date
		Verify Call No.
	STAFF USE ONLY	Other Location (See Message)
	Message	Missing in Inventory
Last Name	Dk. Att. # ☐ CCF ☐	.... Date

A Main Reading Room call slip. The John Adams Building uses a similar one but it is color coded.

INSTRUCTIONS TO READERS

1. Consult catalogs. Print clearly all required information on call slip. Be sure to press firmly enough for good legibility on all copies of this slip.

2. If you need assistance in completing this call slip or in identifying the material you need, please consult a staff member at the Central Desk.

3. When you have completed this form, please submit it to a Book Service Assistant at the Central Desk, who will review the slip for completeness and return the last copy to you to keep.

4. If the call slip is returned to you marked "NOT ON SHELF" you may consult a Book Service Assistant at the Central Desk regarding a further search.

5. Call numbers beginning with the letters, E,G,H,J,P, and F 1200+ are in the Thomas Jefferson Building; use the Main Reading Room for fastest delivery. Those beginning with A,B,C,D,L,N,Q,R,S,T,U,V,Z, and F below 1200 are housed in the John Adams Building; use the Thomas Jefferson Reading Room located on the fifth floor of the John Adams Building for fastest delivery.

LIBRARY OF CONGRESS

71-19 (rev 9/79)

index

179